From Mesopotamia to Iraq

From Mesopotamia to Iraq
A Concise History

Hans J. Nissen and Peter Heine
Translated by Hans J. Nissen

THE UNIVERSITY OF CHICAGO PRESS *Chicago and London*

Hans J. Nissen is professor of ancient Near Eastern archaeology at the Free University of Berlin.

Peter Heine is professor of Near Eastern studies at Humboldt University in Berlin.

The University of Chicago Press, Chicago 60637
The University of Chicago Press, Ltd., London
© 2009 by The University of Chicago
All rights reserved. Published 2009
Printed in the United States of America

Originally published as *Von Mesopotamien zum Irak: Kleine Geschichte eines alten Landes,* by Hans J. Nissen and Peter Heine © 2003 Verlag Klaus Wagenbach, Berlin.

18 17 16 15 14 13 12 11 10 09   1 2 3 4 5

ISBN-13: 978-0-226-58663-2 (cloth)
ISBN-10: 0-226-58663-4 (cloth)
ISBN-13: 978-0-226-58664-9 (paper)
ISBN-10: 0-226-58664-2 (paper)

Library of Congress Cataloging-in-Publication Data

Nissen, Hans J.
    [Von Mesopotamien zum Irak. English]
    From Mesopotamia to Iraq : a concise history /
    Hans J. Nissen and Peter Heine; translated by
Hans J. Nissen.
        p.   cm.
    Includes bibliographical references and index.
    ISBN-13: 978-0-226-58663-2 (cloth : alk. paper)
    ISBN-13: 978-0-226-58664-9 (pbk. : alk. paper)
    ISBN-10: 0-226-58663-4 (cloth : alk. paper)
    ISBN-10: 0-226-58664-2 (pbk. : alk. paper)
    1. Iraq—History—To 634.   2. Iraq—
Civilization—To 634.   I. Heine, Peter.   II. Title.
    DS71.N5713 2009
    956.7—dc22
                                          2008051323
♾ The paper used in this publication meets the minimum requirements of the American National Standard for Information Sciences Permanence of Paper for Printed Library Materials, ANSI Z39.48-1992.

Contents

Preface

In April 2003, the world watched in horror as part of Iraq's cultural heritage disintegrated among the rubble of Saddam Hussein's regime. Looters descended on the Iraq National Museum in Baghdad, Arabic manuscripts disappeared from the National Library, and countless Iraqi government records were destroyed. For those to whom Iraq meant only terror, weapons of mass destruction, or oil, several thousand years of history between the Tigris and the Euphrates opened into view. Basic techniques and concepts of civilization, without which human society would not have attained its present level, had their origin there. A writing system, the prerequisite of modern and premodern societies, was part of the human knowledge that spread from Mesopotamia, as were bureaucratic techniques such as archiving, still basic to any modern administration, or early forms of monotheism. Such "firsts" will be highlighted in the following pages. But the uniqueness of the ancient Mesopotamian culture rests not only on countless innovations of this kind but, to an even greater degree, on the fact that we can follow its gradual development and its absorption into the cultural canon over a period of ten thousand years, almost without major gaps.

The recent catastrophe has therefore affected not only a city or a nation but the whole world, irrespective of the way various societies have developed historically. An important part of the cultural memory and heritage of humankind was lost during the invasion of Iraq, even though a number of antiquities have been recovered which were thought to be lost forever. The failure to guard these treasures remains a disgrace not only for the invaders but even for those who despised Saddam's political and societal system.

The general shock following the looting and destruction of the art and documents from Ur and Nineveh, from Babylon and Ctesiphon, indicates that many people attach greater significance to Mesopotamia than to other countries in the Middle East, even those with histories as long as Mesopotamia's. This is the more remarkable because scholarly interest has focused less on modern Iraq than on countries like Egypt or Lebanon. That the political and military events in Iraq have drawn such attention suggests that they touch deep layers of cultural identity. The disapproval of a preemptive strike against Iraq voiced throughout Europe resulted less from timidity in dealing with conflicts than from a profound awareness of Iraq as a part of the ancient world where some of the basic rules of human coexistence had been formulated for the first time.

In hardly any other continuously inhabited part of the globe can we trace developments in politics, economy, and culture over such an extended time. Both the geographical position of Iraq and its oil have created conflicting interests among foreign powers. In this context we seek to highlight the historical facts that made Iraq and our world what they are today.

1 Landscape, Climate, Population

The name "Mesopotamia" (from the Greek, "between the rivers") was coined by the Romans for the area between the Euphrates and the Tigris, which for some centuries was Rome's easternmost province. Though the area then included part of today's Syria, "Mesopotamia" now is widely used to denote the territory of Iraq within its modern confines. The vast plains formed partly by the alluvial fill of the rift valley separating the African and the Eurasian tectonic sheets characterize the landscape. Mesopotamia includes the western foothills of the huge range of the Zagros Mountains, pushed up by those sheets. The Tigris follows an almost straight course through the original valley, while the Euphrates, having originated in almost the same area as the Tigris, joins this valley only after a wide loop through modern Syria. Ultimately the two rivers flow jointly into the Persian Gulf, the lower part of the valley. For millennia, the sediments carried by the rivers gradually filled the valley, forming a vast alluvial plain. We assume that this process ended about ten thousand years ago, though minor changes may have occurred later.

The filling occurred at irregular intervals: during relatively warm periods, abundant precipitation in the source areas caused the rivers to carry more water and consequently more debris and sediment than during cooler phases. These major or minor changes, however many there were, occurred in times when nonsedentary humans were hardly affected. A shift to a slightly cooler climate in the course of the fourth millennium BCE, however, had a major impact on subsequent development. Around 2000 BCE, the climate

FIGURE 1. Iraq and its neighbors

seems to have settled down to conditions not much different from what we have now.

One of the more important climatic differences within Iraq is that the northern and eastern parts receive enough rain for plants to flourish, while the western and southern parts never have enough for crop cultivation. To be sure, water may be diverted from the rivers, but wide areas in west are beyond the reach of irrigation schemes. The potential fertility of the region becomes evident when a spring rain transforms steppe and desert into a carpet of flowers.

Climatic changes have shifted the border between cultivable and uncultivable areas, but it is unlikely that the southern alluvial plain, or any part of it, ever lay in the rain-fed area. The agriculture of Babylonia—as we shall call, after its later political capital Babylon, the area between modern Baghdad and the head of the Persian Gulf—always had to rely on artificial irrigation. Assyria, or the northern part of modern Iraq, could largely do without.

Most early civilizations, such as the Egyptian, the Chinese, or the Indian, are centered on mighty rivers. In describing, so we might apply to other cultures Egypt as "the gift of the Nile," Herodotus was alluding to the fact that the Nile deposits its fertile sediment on the land just before the sowing season, guaranteeing a high yield every year without the need to fertilize artificially or to let the land lie fallow. But Mesopotamia and the Indus Valley lack that advantage, because in these regions the rivers overflow only when they pose a great danger to the harvest. While the Nile flows south to north, the twin rivers of Mesopotamia, like the Indus, flow in the opposite direction. Since these rivers run high as a result of melting snow and ice in their catchment basins, the melting phase in Ethiopia occurs much earlier in the year than it does in southeastern Anatolia, the source of the Euphrates and the Tigris. Still, there can be no doubt that only abundant water in the rivers enabled the intensive agriculture so essential for early civilizations. In Mesopotamia, the positive use of water had to be wrested from nature, a task that presented no small challenge for Mesopotamian society.

Because the plains had been formed by sedimentation, the terrain offered no raw materials such as metal; nor, at least in the south, was there was any usable stone. The only exception was a spot on the southwestern Euphrates close to the modern city of Samawa, where limestone is found close to the surface. Its inferior quality, however, prevented its use for vessels or ornaments, and only during a brief period in the fourth millennium BCE was it used for building purposes: slabs of limestone form the lower parts of walls of the so-called Limestone Temple in Uruk. Nowadays, this limestone is quarried for cement. It is found here because the parallel chains of the Zagros extend below the flood plain, their peaks occasionally reaching close to the present surface. Unlike the south, the northern and eastern areas have plenty of stone. Of particular interest is a fine-grained alabaster from the northeastern mountains, which was used in neo-Assyrian palaces for the colossal bulls guarding the entrances and for the reliefs covering the walls.

Both building material and technique always pertained to what was possible within a particular region. Thus, stone and especially wood were used in the northern and eastern areas, while brick drawn from the local soil, whether sun-dried or, less often, fired, was used in the alluvial plains. Stone of various colors and hardness, used for jewelry and vessels, came primarily from the Zagros Mountains. One example was carnelian, a semiprecious stone used widely to create beads of all shapes. Lapis lazuli, highly valued for its vivid blueness, was brought from Badakhshan, the northeasternmost valley in modern Afghanistan. Obsidian, from which knives and vessels were made in early times, came from Anatolia. Both precious and normal metals were mined at different places in different periods. Unfortunately, we can only speculate about their origin, because metal objects and fragments were constantly melted down and the original components mixed up with each other. It is impossible to establish links to particular sources. Large quantities of copper probably came mainly from southeastern Anatolia and/ or the Oman Peninsula, but as for the tin used in the production of bronze, we have no idea where it came from. Silver was found in the Zagros ranges, while the question of where gold was found remains unanswered.

Oil was discovered only in modern times, but asphalt, a derivative of oil, has been used in large quantities for five and a half thousand years. It served as the background material for inlay, with colored stones and shell representing figurative scenes and arranged as geometric ornaments; it was probably also used as fuel to reach the high temperatures necessary for metalwork; and from the middle of the third millennium BCE onward we find it used as mortar for bricks, particularly when these are exposed to water, as in drains or bathroom floors. At various spots on the middle Euphrates, primarily in the vicinity of modern (and ancient) Hit, asphalt (*ittu* in the Akkadian language) seeped out of the ground. It found its way into the Euphrates and was collected in lumps downstream.

We will never know the names of all those who participated in the emergence and transformation of the civilizations on Iraqi land. Even for periods with an abundance of written sources we normally only know the main actors. With a certain regularity, new groups arrived, often of a totally different ethnic background. They came as conquerors or as immigrants, sometimes swarming in, sometimes gradually mingling with the existing inhabitants. Unlike the Nile valley with its steep cliffs serving as natural borders, Mesopotamia is open on all sides. Although positive evidence for the arrival of new groups stems only from the time of written information, we can be sure that immigration into Mesopotamia has been going on from time immemorial.

Even the earliest written documents do not reveal the ethnic composition of the population at the time. While meticulously recording economic data, these texts make no effort to transpose spoken language into writing. They could probably be read by speakers of any of the then-current languages. Unable to this day to identify the language behind these texts, we are still at a loss when it comes to naming the people who by the fourth millennium BCE had created an urban civilization in southern Mesopotamia. We may plausibly assume, however, that a major role was played by the Sumerians, whom we can identify seven hundred years later as the moving spirits of Mesopotamian society.

Only around the middle of the third millennium BCE was the writing system transformed so as to render spoken language. At this point, documents and official inscriptions were written in Sumerian. However, in addition to loanwords from Semitic Akkadian, a number of words appear not to belong to any of the known languages. For place-names in particular, such as Uruk, Ur, and Kish, intense scholarly research has yielded no convincing Sumerian etymologies. They probably have to be considered remnants of the languages of the indigenous people settling in the alluvial plain before the massive immigration of the fourth millennium BCE. This mixture of languages indicates that a number of ethnic groups had been living together for a substantial span of time. The period when documents were written in Sumerian lasted only about two hundred years. When Sargon of Akkad, a member of the Semitic population, came to power around 2350 BCE, the language used in nearly all written documents shifted to Semitic Akkadian, using the same cuneiform system. After a century and a half, the pendulum swung back to the Sumerian language, and only after another century and a half did the Semitic languages finally prevail. The temporarily ousted language had obviously not died but continued to be spoken. We cannot safely attribute an Akkadian speaker to the Akkadian ethnic group, for a number of cases were recorded where fathers with a Sumerian name had sons with Akkadian names and vice versa. In spite of a rich written tradition, we still have not determined the actual composition of the population. Sumerian as a spoken language probably disappeared around 2000 BCE.

From the beginning of the second millennium BCE, there was

a constant influx of new immigrant groups. The first groups were ethnically of Semitic affiliation; they entered Mesopotamia in waves and adapted the cuneiform system to their needs, the Akkadians having taken the first transformative step of developing the writing system for their Semitic language. Differences in the written record allow us to differentiate a Babylonian from an Assyrian dialect, corresponding to the southern and northern parts of Mesopotamia. Both the arrival of the Amorites at the beginning at the second millennium BCE, and of the Aramaeans at the beginning of the first, led to substantial changes in the principal Semitic language of Mesopotamia. The next wave of Semitic groups, the Arabs, arrived too late to exercise any influence on the so-called cuneiform languages.

Another important group, the Hurrians—for some time constituting the major portion of the northern Mesopotamian population—were notable both for adapting the cuneiform script to their own language and for producing, through their influence on the Akkadian language, a locally confined Hurrito-Akkadian dialect.

Finally, we should mention those groups whose existence has been recorded but who left little imprint on the written language. Among these were the Kassites, who in the second half of the second millennium formed a major part of the population of Babylonia and for a couple of centuries even provided the political leadership. The same is true of those groups who, during the force relocation of entire populations, had been resettled in Mesopotamia.

For thousands of years, members of all those groups have been living in the same country and intermarrying. To trace any one group in modern Iraq back to its origins is virtually impossible. Rather, we should see precisely these immigrations and amalgamations of ethnic groups as having shaped Mesopotamian civilization in all its liveliness and variety.

2 The Beginnings of Sedentary Life

(Ca. 10,000–4000 BCE)

Until about twelve thousand years ago, the way of life in the Near East, the Eastern Mediterranean, and other parts of Europe was roughly comparable. About thirty thousand years ago, groups of Neanderthalers (*Homo sapiens neanderthalensis*) preferred to roam in areas where the climate supported a wide variety of game and edible plants and fruits, so a sojourn could be extended to the maximum length of time. The Neanderthalers' existence in the Near East is proved by traces and remains found in several caves, including caves in Mount Carmel in present-day Israel, the Beldibi Cave in Southeastern Anatolia, and the Hotu Cave in the Iranian Elburz mountains. The cave of Shanidar in northeastern Iraq acquired fame when excavators there found flowers strewn over a human burial, which was taken as early evidence of belief in an afterlife.

From about 10,000 BCE onward, there are hints that the Near East was developing differently from neighboring regions, as evidenced by the first appearance of domesticated plants and animals and of dwellings that were more than natural shelters or sheds.

Some two thousand years earlier, the situation had changed substantially. According to DNA analyses, modern man (*Homo sapiens sapiens*) had found his way from East Africa to the Near East, where he encountered Neanderthalers. Though they lived side by side for long periods, their coexistence ended in total victory for modern man.

The Neanderthalers must have been ousted long before 10,000 BCE, since sedentism and domestication were introduced by modern man from the very beginning. It is unclear what triggered

BCE	Periods	Characteristics	Rulers
8000	Aceramic Neolithic	Domestication of plants and animals; first permanent settlements in ecologically diversified areas	
7000			
6500	Ceramic Neolithic	Settlements in rain-fed areas within and at the fringes of mountain ranges; far-reaching trade; specialized settlements	
6000	Hassuna		
5500	Samarra		
5000	Halaf	Emergence of local centers	
4500	Ubaid	Beginning of urban structures	
4000	Early Uruk	Start of the massive occupation of the southern Mesopotamian alluvium from the neighboring areas	
3500	Late Uruk	Emergence of urban center/city-states in southern Mesopotamia with writing, art, and monumental architecture	
3000	Djemdet Nasr	Beginning of large-scale canal systems	Gilgamesh
2500	Early Dynastic	Emergence of regional states	Urnanshe
	Akkad	1st central state of the Dynasty of Akkad	Sargon
2000	Ur III	Central state of the IIIrd Dynasty of Ur	Urnamma
	Old Assyrian	Assyrian trade colonies in Asia Minor	
	Old Babylonian	Central state of the Ist Dynasty of Babylon	Hammurapi
1500	Kassites/Middle Assyrian	Kassite Dynasties	Kurigalzu Asur-uballit I
1000	Neo-Assyrian	Neo-Assyrian Empire	Assurnasirpal II Assurbanipal
	Chaldeans	Chaldean Empire	Nebuchadnezzar II
500	Achaemenids	Achaemenid Empire	Darius I Alexander
CE			
0	Seleucids		Antiochus I Soter
	Parthians		Mithridates
	Sasanians		Ardashir Shapur II
500		Islamic Conquest of Mesopotamia	

FIGURE 2. Chronology of Mesopotamia, 8000 BCE to 500 CE

the development of sedentary life. Perhaps the greater intellectual flexibility that enabled early humans to assert themselves against the Neanderthalers also helped them to recognize problems and find solutions. The basic idea may have been to remain as long as possible in areas that had proved favorable. Finding a suitable place to stay included careful selection of the campsite; besides easy access to water it was imperative that the environment should be topographically differentiated and rich in species. With variation in microclimate and land level, such an environment would comprise a wide range of plants with different ripening periods, augmented by an abundance of fish, fowl, and game.

Even more important for success was the ability to store food, so as to guarantee survival when hunting and gathering did not suffice because of weather or the exhaustion of what nature had to offer. Reserves had to be built up, beyond the daily needs, but such reserves could be relied on only after food had been produced systematically. Existing knowledge of the reproductive behavior of animals and of the growing cycle of plants was put to use by keeping animals in herds and by cultivating a variety of plants. In this way, more food than was needed for daily consumption would be acquired, and the surplus could be stored.

There are several reasons why sedentism started earlier in the Near East than in other areas with similar environmental conditions. First, conditions like the ones just mentioned are found throughout the mountainous regions of the Taurus and Zagros mountains. Second, and equally decisive, these mountain ranges were the original home of a number of animals and plants (fig. 3) which, with human manipulation, produced higher yields or became more usable. The best example is the sheep, which in its wild form is covered with thick hair like a goat. It was only domestication that allowed an increase in the number of mutants that bore only the woolen undercoat. This increase made possible the breeding of wool sheep, an innovation that gradually spread over the entire world. Not only sheep but goats, cattle, and pigs were also maintained in herds. As for crops, the primary ones, in addition to lentils and peas, were cereals such as einkorn, emmer, wheat, and barley.

Both herding and agriculture are frequently afflicted with epi-

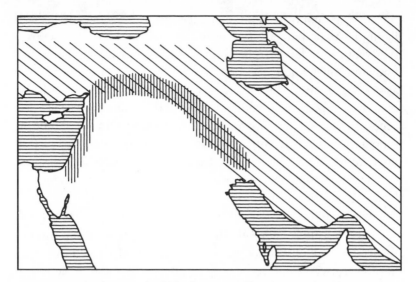

FIGURE 3. Distribution of wild barley (vertical hatching) and wild sheep

demics, crop failure, or other misfortunes. Because of this inherent unreliability, the main diet continued to be based on hunting, fishing, and gathering, while cultivation and domestic animals merely offered an extra, if welcome, source of food. In case of disaster, a full-scale return to hunting and gathering was always possible. With this kind of mixed economy, early settlements had to command enough territory to supply all their needs. Requiring such large areas, settlements in this period tended to be widely separated so as not to infringe on neighboring territories.

These early settlers increasingly sought to replace the uncertainty of food gathering by the relative security of food production. The former option gradually lost importance. Thus the need to control large territories lessened, which in turn allowed settlements to draw closer to each other.

This course of events, though spread over a long period, marks the most important step in the early development of Mesopotamia. The new forms of organization, however, started as options that could be abandoned if necessary, whether because of the problems involved in food production, or because the less secure but also less demanding life of hunting and gathering was found more attrac-

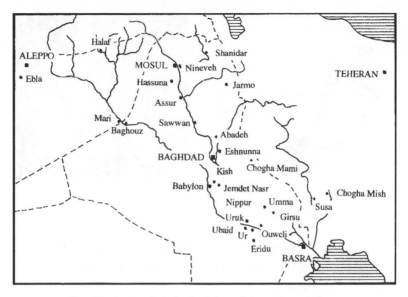

FIGURE 4. Near Eastern archaeological sites of the early periods

tive. To reduce the risk of natural disaster, these early cultivators had to refine their production techniques. A major attempt to enhance productivity was to supply extra water to the fields.

The first settlements had been far enough apart from each other to prevent conflict between neighbors. With greater dependence on cultivation, things changed. Once the settlers had abandoned the large territories surrounding their individual settlement, they could no longer return to the mode of food gathering, thus making the development irreversible. The diminishing distances between settlements created the possibility of neighboring conflicts. With an increasingly safe supply of food, the population and the size of settlements grew, and conflicts increased not only between but also within settlements.

Even among bands of hunters and gatherers, some kind of hierarchy and leadership structures had existed. In the new settlements, rules for conflict avoidance and conflict management called for new structures to monitor the rules and to inflict sanctions in case of violation. As these structures were granted legitimacy, a new quality of leadership emerged.

Settlements of the eighth and seventh millennia BCE have been

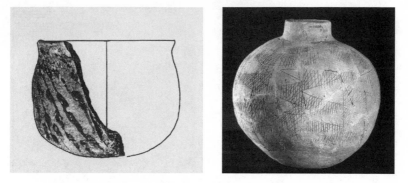

FIGURE 5. Decorated pottery vessels, ca. 6000 BCE, from Qal'at Jarmo (height: 9 cm), and Tell Hassuna (height: 40 cm)

excavated in small numbers and in limited sections only. From the shape, size, and arrangement of the houses there is not enough evidence to draw inferences on economic or social aspects. Nor can we draw any conclusions about political-religious leadership by looking at public buildings. In particular, all religious events or ideas are totally out of our reach, in spite of their probable dominance over most aspects of life.

Only the increasing need for storage containers is indicative of a more complex economy. In earlier periods, wood, leather, and stone had been used for containers. Now all kinds of malleable materials came to be used, including clay, though ceramic vessels were not manufactured this early. It was a long time before people realized that clay could meet the growing demand of containers more efficiently and easily than anything else.

The large-scale production of pottery vessels started in the seventh millennium BCE, marking both a technological and an economic advance. Furthermore, it gives us greater access to the witnesses of the past. From the beginning, pottery vessels were more than containers. Different ways of treating their surface turned them into a medium for creating identities. An inexhaustible range of patterns and motifs could be incised or painted on vessels to represent membership and definition.

Since shapes as well as decoration were subject to fashion and technological changes, pottery vessels, even in the form of sherds, can be attributed to specific periods or areas. For periods preceding the occurrence of written documents or artworks, pottery provides the most reliable means of archaeological dating. That is why the various periods, which together constitute a very long time span, between the emergence of pottery and the first appearance of written historical documents are named after specific pottery groups—and these usually bear the names of those sites where the pottery was first identified, such as "Ubaid" after the site of Tell el-Ubaid in southern Iraq, "Halaf" after Tell Halaf in Syria, or "Samarra" after the city in northern Iraq.

The use of pottery for chronological purposes depends largely on the excavation of sites that were occupied for very long periods, where occupational debris, including pottery sherds, accumulated in a series of layers. Analyzing the contents of one layer only allows dating relative to another layer. The time distance to our own day can be determined only if a specific point within a pottery sequence can be subjected to either carbon-14 analysis or tree-ring dating (dendrochronology).

Fortunately, we know quite a number of such long-lived settlements. In most cases, the time levels are easy to separate, because ancient Near Eastern architecture left thick layers of residential remains. Ever since solid buildings were first erected, clay or mud had been used as the main building material, either by stacking up layers of mud on site, or by using mud bricks. In both cases the mud was only sun-dried. Consequently, both rain and wind dissolved such walls into the original components. While both plaster and regular care might prevent rapid decay, the lifetime of an ordinary house could hardly be extended beyond one or two generations. If a house was not worth repairing, all reusable materials, as as roof beams or doors, were ripped out (fig. 6). The remainder was left to decay. The debris formed a thick layer of mud, which eventually would be leveled off before being used as a new building lot. This process having been repeated many times within the lifetime of a settlement, the ruins of ancient cities in the Near East tend to consist of a sequence of thick layers.

We still do not know much about settlement buildings in the early pottery periods of the seventh millennium BCE. As far as economics is concerned, it is interesting to note that the settlers felt a need to mark property and to use mnemonic devices to store num-

FIGURE 6. Abandoned village in southern Iraq (1966 photograph)

FIGURE 7. Stamp seal from the sixth millennium BCE

bers or amounts. Seals (fig. 7) were used to stamp property marks on the clay lids or fasteners of all kinds of containers, while clay tokens in various simple shapes (fig. 8) stood for specific numerical values. Obviously it was thought necessary to store information for later checking.

An excavation site at Tell es-Sawwan, within the Early Islamic Abbasid city complex of Samarra on the left embankment of the Tigris, offers insight into the structure of a sixth-millennium settlement (fig. 9). When the settlement had been totally uncovered, ten freestanding building complexes of the same size were found,

FIGURE 8. Simple clay counting devices

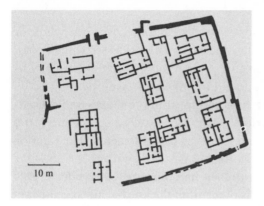

10 m

FIGURE 9. Plan of
Tell es-Siwwan, sixth
millennium BCE

surrounded by an almost quadrangular system of wall and moat. None of the houses stands out from the others by size, layout, or furnishing, so that it might be identified as the house of a leading figure. If there was any leadership structure, it did not manifest itself in a way that could be traced archaeologically. Samarra-ware, the pottery named after this site, has been found distributed over a large area: from the surroundings of Mosul (Hassuna) to the area where the Euphrates meets Iraqi territory (Baghouz) and to the first chains of the Zagros to the east (Chogha Mami). Since other, similar layouts of houses have been uncovered, as well as similar human and animal figurines, we can justifiably speak of a cultural unit (or, in short, a "culture").

These characteristics become even more apparent if compared with the roughly contemporary Halaf culture. Again, internal similarities encompass pottery, human and animal figurines, seals and amulets, and houses of a specific shape: round, with a rectangular

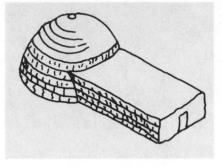

FIGURE 10. A round house of the Halaf period (suggested reconstruction), sixth millennium BCE

antechamber (fig. 10). The area of distribution covers the whole of Syria, southeastern Anatolia, and Mesopotamia as far as the Tigris. In other words, Halaf culture is more or less complementary to Samarra culture, overlapping it in only a few aspects.

The most striking differences appear in the shapes and decoration of pottery. The exteriors of Samarra vessels display concentric, frequently broken lines and bands as basic elements. The interior decoration of open bowls often consists of swirling motifs—for example, human figures with their hair blowing to one side. Vessels were handmade, with walls of medium thickness. Painting appears to have been in a single color but shadings caused by the firing process can be seen. The surface of the pottery is mat (fig. 11a).

Halaf pottery, on the other hand, in addition to concentric lines, includes self-contained patterns that divide the surface into individual fields rather than emphasizing the vessel's curvature (fig. 11b). Through the intentional use of different paints as well as color shading caused by firing, a multicolored appearance is produced. This pottery too was handmade. In addition to normal pottery shapes, particular vessels have been found that are oval or rectangular in form or that were designed in a fanciful mode with high, funnel-shaped rims. These special forms often have extremely thin walls, making one wonder how they remained intact when fired.

The most striking feature of these vessels is the high shine of their surface. This was accomplished neither by polishing nor by any other external treatment but by a complicated process of

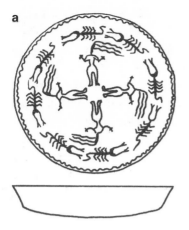

FIGURE II. Vessels of the Samarra culture (sixth millennium BCE), the Halaf culture (sixth millennium BCE), and the Ubaid culture (fifth millennium BCE)

preparing the painting material and controlling the firing. For the painting, a very fine clay was used containing iron oxides, which reacted differently during the firing. The clay was treated with water until only the finest parts of it remained—something like the process resulting in the shiny surface of puddles as they dry up after rain. The microscopic scales form a coating and thus produce the shiny effect—a technique similar to the one used later by the Greeks for their red- and black-figured vases. The significant differences between Samarra and Halaf pottery production point to a wide separation in technology. Taking the dissimilarities in architecture into account, we get a picture of two fundamentally different cultural units.

The central plains running from Syria to southwestern Iran appear to have been occupied by two large cultural units, which maintained a clear separation from each other. We do not know, however, whether this separation reflects both ethnic and cultural differences, or whether the respective internal similarities point to joint structures in the areas of religion or politics.

Despite their differences, these units have many features in common. Neither one shows any traces of specific buildings that could be singled out as public or communal buildings or temples. Furthermore, during the following period both units were integrated into what is known as the Ubaid culture, again defined by a pottery style (fig. 11c). Besides its signature pottery, Ubaid favored a highly characteristic house form with a large central hall (fig. 12). Pottery production was enhanced by the use of a new technical aid, the turntable. It wasn't long before these two features spread over what had been both the Samarra and the Halaf territories, suggesting that they answered needs shared by both groups.

With the help of a horizontal turntable that could be revolved around a central spike at its base for the manufacture of vessels, the decorative patterns assumed a characteristic form, consisting almost exclusively of concentric bands and other ornamentation. The bands resulted when a brush was held against the vessel as it turned. Decorative elements between the bands, such as wavy lines or garlands, were produced by light touches of the brush.

The turntable both simplified and accelerated production. It demonstrated that pottery making, at least to some degree, had become a profession. Where this new technology originated is not known; it could have been anywhere in what is now Iraq.

In private houses, the various functional rooms were usually distinct from the space used for connecting the rooms. In "the house with a central hall" (fig. 12), on the other hand, the hall is used both as the main living area—as shown by the fireplace—and as the main connecting area between the rooms along either side. This arrangement points to a new way of organizing domestic life. As in the case of pottery production, this new scheme was apparently found attractive enough to be accepted in the entire area of former Samarra and Halaf. Both phenomena strongly suggest the existence of a communication network covering most of the Near East by this period at the latest.

The subsequent development toward early urban life is domi-

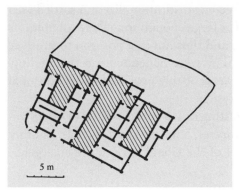

FIGURE 12. Plan of a house with a large central hall at Tell Abadeh, Ubaid period (fifth millennium BCE)

nated by two key concepts: the *central place* and the *central function*. A settlement is designated a central place when, in addition to being larger (or usually so) and containing more special elements than other settlements, it possesses features that serve not only its own inhabitants but also those in the surrounding settlements. These central functions are what make a settlement into an administrative, religious, or political center. Because of the systematic relations between the central place and the surrounding settlements, we use the term "settlement system."

The earliest examples of the institutionalization of central functions in the form of public buildings are found in the Ubaid period. We take such buildings to indicate an increasingly complex society. They are identified by the excavators either as "temples" (Eridu) or as "palaces" (Ouweli), at any rate as the seat of a religious or political authority; no more details are available.

By and large, early settlement had focused on mountainous or hilly zones. It was only during the Ubaid period that settlers took over the large central plains, formerly occupied only sparsely. Settlements such as Susa or Chogha Mish in Khuzestan for the first time constitute central places which, by location, size, and surrounding settlements, prove to be the highest segment of three-tiered settlement systems: ranged below them we find a number of smaller centers, which in turn are the points of reference for settlements on the lowest level. Whether it is already appropriate to speak of "cities" or "urban centers" is a matter of definition, but there is clear indication that certain public tasks and some social differentiation have become institutionalized. A settled area of about twenty hectares was large enough to include inhabitants charged with public service and thus not in a position to produce their own food. For that, they were dependent on their fellow citizens. The central place was probably provided with additional food supplied by the countryside.

It would have been interesting to see how this kind of organization might have developed further, but it was overtaken by another process heralded by the end of the Ubaid period: the emergence of urban civilization.

3 The First Urban Society and the Use of Writing

(Ca. 4000–3200 BCE)

Between the ninth and the fourth millennia BCE, complex forms of human existence developed much more rapidly in the Near East than in other parts of the world. Despite local differences, the general development of major parts of the Near East seems to have taken the same course at approximately the same pace during the periods discussed so far. This parallel advancement was to cease during the fourth millennium, for southern Mesopotamia was about to step out of line and to pursue a course of its own. In that region, the first urban society emerged within the relatively short period of three or four hundred years prior to 3200 BCE.

Unfortunately, the seven or eight hundred years between the end of the Ubaid period and the end of Late Uruk (as the period immediately preceding 3200 is called), rates among the worst documented times of the history of the ancient Near East. Almost everywhere, remains of this period are buried beneath several meters of later deposits. Traces have been found only in deep soundings, which were sunk into the many layers of settlement debris to establish the sequence of levels and the date of the earliest occupation. Merely exposing these levels, however, was sufficient to ascertain their existence.

For the time around 3200, the picture is entirely different, because extensive information has been derived from the ancient city of Uruk (fig. 13), where the German Archaeological Institute has been conducting excavations for almost forty years. A large area in the center of the city provides a window for archaeologists, who have been able to recover remains from the time around 3200 fairly close to the surface. Most of what we know about

FIGURE 13.
Plan of the city
of Uruk. The
hatched area
was occupied in
3200 BCE; and
the city wall
dates from ca.
2900 BCE.

this time was found in Uruk, which appropriately lent its name to
the period. Additional information was secured by archaeological investigation in the hinterland of the city. Location, size, and
date of all the ancient settlements were incorporated into maps,
enabling scholars to study changes in settlement patterns. Finally,
the investigations mentioned earlier, which sought evidence of climatic changes over time, further contributed to evaluating the
significance of this period.

Good information on a number of different aspects allows us
to paint a relatively coherent picture. We can even draw conclusions on the preceding period, which offers no evidence of itself.
New structures in different areas had emerged after the end of the
Ubaid, far outstripping the Ubaid structures, which had already
attained a level of complexity. Around 3200, the settlement of
Uruk itself covered more than ten times the area of the largest
settlements in the Ubaid period. Impressive artworks, large and
differentiated public areas, and, not least, the earliest script indicate
such a remarkable leap in all areas as to undermine the assumption
of a continuous, steady development. The antiquities in Uruk were

so accessible and so plentiful because major parts of the central area had been left relatively unused between the middle of the third millennium and the seventh century BCE, that is, for about two thousand years.

The center of the city consisted of two large public areas; one of these was surrounded by a wall of its own, whereas the other may or may not have been walled (fig. 13; but see also chap. 4, fig. 31, left). Around 3200, Uruk covered an area of at least 250 hectares, or about one square mile (conservatively estimated), with between twenty-five thousand and fifty thousand inhabitants. Presumably, this area was surrounded by a city wall, which during the following period was buried under new construction as the city grew. The two central areas are the only reminder that Uruk was formed from two settlements lying on either side of the Euphrates. No doubt the river could be forded here without major effort. By 3200, however, the two settlements had long since grown together.

The two central areas had probably been the cultic centers of the former settlements. They were organized on opposite principles. The western area—dubbed Anu District because Anu, the god of heaven was worshipped there later—was arranged around a terrace eleven meters high, serving as foundation for a temple six meters high, its plaster painted white—hence the name White Temple (fig. 14). Extensive building activities during the first millennium BCE left many meters of debris covering the ground surrounding the terrace, which has prevented us from gaining detailed information.

The eastern area is known by its later name of Eanna, being the cultic center for the worship of Inanna, the goddess of Uruk. When an area about three hundred by two hundred meters square was excavated, central Eanna was found to include a number of different buildings within its own surrounding wall. No clearly central structure was apparent. Instead, several buildings of as large as fifty-four by twenty meters square were found, surrounded by buildings of different layouts and measurements, indicating that they had served different functions (fig. 15).

What basically differentiates the White Temple from the buildings in Eanna is relative size, which determined the number of people who could take part in whatever happened in those buildings. While the central space of the White Temple could accommo-

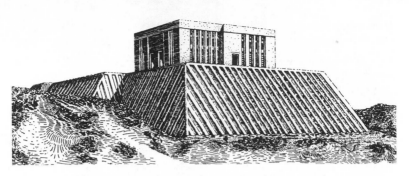

FIGURE 14. The White Temple in Uruk (E. Heinrich's suggested reconstruction), ca. 3200 BCE

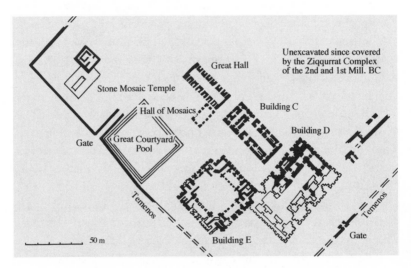

FIGURE 15. Excavated part of the central Eanna area of Uruk, 3200 BCE (Archaic Level IVa)

date ten to fourteen persons—if that indeed was its purpose—the central hall of Building C in Eanna could seat three hundred. If both buildings served cultic purposes, the sequence of events or cultic acts must have followed different rules. On the other hand, the large buildings in Eanna may not have served cultic purposes but may have been functioned in relation to city government.

There is another reason why we may never find out what happened there. The buildings in Eanna were not destroyed but were deliberately dismantled, probably as part of an encompassing ar-

FIGURE 16. Reception hall of a modern sheikh's residence in southern Iraq, made of reed bundles and woven reed (1966 photograph)

chitectural and organizational restructuring of the area. They were carefully emptied before the walls were taken down, leaving wall stumps only thirty to fifty centimeters high. No cultic vessel was left behind, no drinking bowl that might give us a hint of what was going on there. Only the fireplaces in the central halls—again carefully cleaned—suggest that rituals may have been performed; but we cannot rule out a very practical purpose: they may simply have served to warm those present during the cold and inhospitable winters.

The Great Hall with its many deep buttresses may have been covered by a vault. Its disproportionate length relative to its width reminds us of the reception halls of sheikhs' residences in southern Iraq close to the present day (fig. 16), and may have served the same purpose.

If even larger numbers of people needed to be accommodated, other solutions had to be found, since the beams available at the time could not have bridged wider spans. This need may have led to Building E, which combines four long halls into a square and could accommodate four times as many people as the rectangular Building C.

Close by and still within the confines of Eanna, a basin forty-nine by forty-five meters across and one and one-half meters deep was found, most likely connected with ritual performances. Also close by and within Eanna, a small building was found, with columns covered by mosaic in intricate patterns, fashioned by multicolored clay cones.

All of these buildings have to be seen in conjunction with central

FIGURE 17. Cylinder seal and modern impression (ca. 3200 BCE)

organizational structures; yet we can perceive no obvious cultic connections. The term "cultic" should no doubt be defined very loosely, for at that time almost every public gathering occurred within the framework of religious concepts. Only a few things may be explained as cultic in a narrow sense.

Among the various functions of Eanna was an economic one. On the one hand, there are remains of what seems to have been a metalworking shop, and there are also thick layers of waste from pottery kilns. More conspicuously, excavation of layers of trash within Eanna has yielded thousands of fragments of clay lids or fasteners stamped with a seal and thousands of clay tablets containing early script. About 80 percent of the written documents bear data of a central economic administration.

As early as in the sixth millennium BCE, clay was used to plug the opening of vessels or to wrap around the knot of bales or sacks so as to protect the contents. The protection could be reinforced if the person responsible impressed his seal onto the clay. Seal impressions indicate the owner of the goods or the person guaranteeing that the contents will not be harmed, and sometimes both. Since seal impressions were supposed to identify the owner of the seal, seal patterns had to be individually distinctive. The more complex the pattern—for instance, by including human or animal representations—the more accurate was the identification.

Unlike the stamp seals of earlier times, seals by about 3200 had attained the shape of small stone cylinders, three to five centimeters long, with all kinds of compositions engraved on their curved surface. They had probably first appeared one or two hundred years earlier. Rolling the cylinder would leave a raised mark on the clay. The curved surface usually far exceeded the size of the

FIGURE 18. Two sides of a clay tablet (6.2 cm × 4.4 cm), ca. 3200 BCE. Sections on the front (left) list numbers of various kinds of sheep and goats. The total number of animals is listed on the back (right).

former stamp seal, so now there was space for engraving complex patterns and an unlimited variety of unique images. Cylinder seals, as well as fragments of fasteners showing impressions of the seals, are clear evidence of economic life in that period.

Clay tablets bear similar witness to an economic administration. By means of wooden or reed styluses, indentations standing for numbers were applied to the surface of these tablets, or signs indicating words were engraved. If, for instance, the animals in a herd had to be listed individually, bold lines divided the surface into compartments, separating the different pieces of information; in this case, the reverse of the tablet could be used to give the total number of animals (fig. 18).

A kind of shorthand, omitting verb forms and prepositions, was used to record details of administrative processes, which consisted primarily of the arrival and departure of goods from the central storehouses. These documents served as memory aid for the administrators, recording only those pieces of information that differed from common knowledge. Lacking such common knowledge, we are at a disadvantage for understanding these texts. Only numbers were written in full, without abbreviations. A mixed sexagesimal-decimal system was in use, with individual signs for

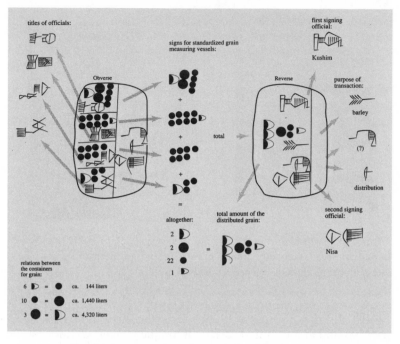

FIGURE 19. Graphic interpretation of an archaic tablet (7.7 × 4.9 cm), ca. 3000 BCE. The front shows the amounts of barley allotted to four high officials. The back shows the total amount issued and the names of the officials.

units ranging between 0.1 and 36,000. (The sexagesimal system, based as it is on the number 60, is the ancestor of the way we tell time, in hours, minutes, and seconds.) Along with general-purpose number systems, others were used for specific commodities, such as—barley (fig. 19).

A wide variety of goods were recorded on the tablets, with food, especially barley, taking the main share. Unfortunately, we never get to know where these goods came from or who delivered them. The same is true of live animals, dairy products such as milk and cheese, and, most regrettably, metals, the provenance of which we would love to know.

A text from the subsequent stage of writing, around 3000 BCE, can be recognized as summarizing deliveries to four individuals who, however, are identified not by name but by their titles, which we happen to know from another context (fig. 19).

Almost 20 percent of the early written material consists not of economic data but of so-called lexical lists: an enumeration of words and concepts from the same semantic family. Some of these documents list the names of animals according to kind, such as cattle, pigs, birds, or fish; others list the names of trees or cities. One particularly interesting document lists titles and professions; in this case we can even recognize the ordering principle, as the entries are arranged hierarchically.

Such lists are among the oldest written documents. They might even have been instrumental in devising the writing system—at least, that could explain their revered status. Not only were they constantly copied and recopied almost without variation during the oldest writing stages, probably as part of scribal education, but the same process continued well into the following centuries, when some of the archaic signs had fallen out of use and were no longer understood.

The first part of the titles and professions list gives us an insight in the structure of political leadership. Although the opening entry has barely survived into subsequent periods, it occurs two thousand years later—around 1200 BCE—in a dictionary of ancient words, where it is translated by the term for king. The precise meaning of "king" in the dictionary is unimportant; the point is that the title is meant to denote the highest official. In loose translation, the next entries in the original, fourth-millennium document list "the leader of law," "the leader of the city," "the leader of barley," "the leader of the plow," "the leader of the labor force," and, a few lines later, "the leader of the assembly." The document reads like the directory of a modern city administration.

We are not surprised to find the head of the judiciary in the list, since large communities need rules and institutions to handle conflicts and to inflict sanctions if necessary. Neither is it surprising to find a leader of the assembly, since the *Gilgamesh Epic* frequently mentions the assembly of city elders who form the opposition to the ruler. To be sure, the epic is a later composition, but in essence it centers on events that happened only a few centuries after the time we are discussing.

So far, no obvious government buildings have been found, though the economic and political administration had to be ac-

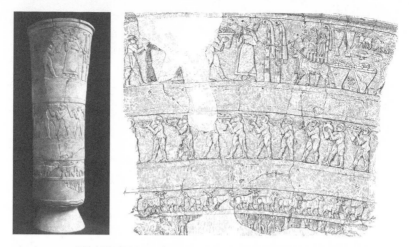

FIGURE 20. The "Cult Vase" from Uruk, ca. 3200–3000 BCE (preserved height: 105 cm)

commodated somewhere. Perhaps that is what the buildings in Eanna were for: the variety of buildings may have corresponded to the multitude of different functions performed there.

On the whole, the society of the time seems to have been ordered hierarchically. In the later part of the list of titles, groups of entries appear, giving different ranks within the same function or profession. In this connection, a workshop, perhaps for metalworking, has been uncovered in Uruk in which the arrangement indicates that a number of workmen performed the same task under a coordinator. Such an arrangement may express a fairly advanced division of labor.

The principle of hierarchy is most visibly expressed on the "Cult Vase from Uruk," which depicts plants and animal as well as humans (fig. 20). The exterior of this fragmentary vessel, which is made of limestone, is covered with four concentric bands of reliefs, increasing in height from the bottom to the top. Above the pedestal, which is decorated with wavy lines symbolizing water, the lowest band presents ears of barley alternating with palm shoots. The next band depicts a row of alternating male and female sheep. The third and fourth bands are reserved for human beings. The third depicts naked men carrying baskets with various agricultural products. The fourth is the first to present a complex composition as the main scene. Although the section containing the main figure is severely damaged, what remains of this figure, as well as comparisons to other compositions, indicates that he was the ruler. He is preceded by a servant carrying offerings, while another servant walks behind him, carrying the ruler's richly decorated train. In the vase's original form, the ruler was depicted taller than the other figures, showing that he was considered the most important person according to the ancient Near Eastern code of representation.

The ruler and his entourage move toward two sheaves of reed, a female figure standing in front of them—though she is probably meant to stand between them. The sheaves are tied at the thin upper parts of the reeds, while the leafy tops hang down like banners. Sheaves of this kind, varying in the shape of the upper part, are known to serve as emblems or standards for a number of cities. They may be read as a sign for either the city or its principal deity. The standards on the Uruk vase stand for the city or for the city goddess Inanna. In this instance, they represent the temple of Inanna, which is shown not as a building but as an array of cult objects assembled inside the temple. Animal figurines on pedestals carry human figurines on their back; also depicted are containers with offerings and two tall vases of the same shape as the cult vase. Clearly, the cult vase itself had been part of the inventory of a temple.

In the composition, the ruler is depicted as performing one of his duties, the worship of the city goddess, who is represented by her high priestess. In scenes on other art objects, again the ruler is the central figure. On the so-called lion-hunting stela (fig. 21), the ruler can be seen twice: in one case he is attacking a lion with a lance, in the other with a bow and arrow. Attacking with a lance manifested special bravery, and hunting lions remained a privilege of rulers into much later times. On cylinder seals we meet frequent variants of a scene in which the ruler supervises his men as they beat shackled prisoners with clubs. Since the prisoners are not identified as foreign, the action depicted may refer to internal problems. On another seal we see the ruler performing yet another

FIGURE 21. Basalt lion-hunt stela from Uruk, ca. 3200–3000 BCE (preserved height: 100 cm)

FIGURE 22. Female head from Uruk, ca. 3200–3000 BCE, limestone (height: 21 cm)

of his duties, the symbolic feeding of animals. The only art object found so far in Uruk that does not depict a ruler is in the form of a female head; fig. 22.

No other figure occupies such a central role in art, and certainly none that we could identify with a cult or a religion. Indeed, in the list of titles and professions we find no unambiguous title for a cultic office. On the other hand, we are clearly in an environment defined by religion, as attested by the common use of the same designation for both the city and its deity. Religion was so much a part of life that it framed all activities without becoming manifest to the extent that visual remnants could be traced.

If we assume that the strict and encompassing hierarchy, notably the structure visible in the titles list, had not existed long before 3200, we understand why the ruler, along with the entire organization he represented, had to be emphasized visually. For this purpose, all the former prerogatives of a chief were employed: the hunt, the use of (internal) force, and cultic duties; but never before had these elements been depicted visually.

A major innovation in this period was the use of an axle and bearings. A shaft was placed between two bearings (which were probably lubricated in some way) such that a tool affixed to it could be set in rapid rotation. Here we encounter another first, the prototype of all rotating tools. We know of at least two tools using this principle at the time.

One of these new tools was the fast potter's wheel, which revolutionized pottery production. The perpendicular axle was affixed to a plate near its upper end, while the lower end moved within a socket. In contrast to the turntable used before, the fast wheel rotated freely, thus allowing vessels to be formed from the clay on the wheel. This procedure laid the groundwork for a technique that appeared a little later, when a number of vessels could be produced, one after the other, from a larger lump of clay, marking the beginning of mass production.

In the Late Uruk period, however, the demand for a huge number of vessels was met in a different way. A bowl with a beveled rim is found by the millions in sites of this period (fig. 23); it was the first mass-produced item in history. The standard type shows little variation and has a capacity of roughly 850 cubic centimeters. Unlike other pottery at the time, these bowls were molded in a form, and the excess clay was cut off with a knife. The material was extremely coarse, tempered with sand—in some places with chaff—and therefore very porous. The beveled-rim bowl probably served for the barley rations that were distributed to the workers

FIGURE 23. Bowl with beveled rim
(upper diameter: approx. 18 cm)
and the writing sign for allotment

FIGURE 24. Writing signs for cart, ca.
3200 BCE

in large economic units, which were organized as households. Although this kind of remuneration is described only several centuries later, a particular writing sign indicates that it may have been practiced as early as 3200: a human head is combined with a bowl set on the lips, meaning "allocation." The double line at the rim attests to a beveled-rim bowl (fig. 23). These bowls were an integral part of an economy of redistribution.

Like the potter's wheel, the other new tool of the period can only be inferred from the marks it left on artifacts it was used for. A wheel made of grinding material was fixed to a horizontal shaft so that it could be rotated rapidly—in other words, a primitive lathe. This tool was used to engrave lines into stone surfaces, especially to outline compositions or to produce geometric patterns on seals. The marks made by the tool are unmistakable: the more or less straight lines fade away at both ends, whereas curved lines thicken at the vertex (see chap. 4, fig. 28).

We do not know where the idea of setting an axle and bearings originated. Whatever it was invented for, it was soon serving other purposes as well, such as the creation of the wagon (fig. 24). In the early models, axle and wheels were presumably attached to each other, the axle turning below the body of the wagon; later the axle was attached to the body, and the wheels turned on the axle. Both the potter's wheel and the lathe obviously served to simplify and speed up the production processes.

The city of Uruk maintained close relations with its hinterland. Its many settlements, large and small, are distributed over the area such that they fall into a four-tiered settlement hierarchy with

Uruk at the top, and then various large settlements, each forming a subcenter of smaller a system, and finally the smallest settlements (see below, fig. 27, right).

The spatial relation of settlements to each other, to their respective subcenters, and to Uruk indicates that they were linked to one another economically and to Uruk both economically and politically. This linkage coincides with the assumption that the inhabitants of Uruk, even if there were only twenty-five thousand, could not produce enough food for themselves and depended on supplies from the countryside. No agricultural area large enough to fill their needs existed in the immediate vicinity of Uruk, which was already occupied by other settlements.Besides, as we have seen, a fairly large number of people were engaged in governing or administrative positions and lacked the time to grow crops or raise animals.

Unfortunately, the texts are silent on the manner in which food was delivered to Uruk or the organizational structures necessary to collect the food from the people who produced it. We may assume, however, that considerable effort was required, expressed perhaps in such titles as "leader of the plowmen," or "leader of the barley (supplies)," which are encountered in the titles list.

Nor do the texts say anything about the provenance of the many raw materials that had to be imported into the country. Such materials included metal, common or semiprecious stone, and timber for wider spans than three or four meters, which could be bridged by local palm trunks. Nothing is known about payment for these goods. Since certain texts refer to a fairly advanced textile industry, textiles may well have been used as exchange goods, as they were in later times.

Single items such as written documents, cylinder seals, or pottery from other places in Babylonia demonstrate that much of what we know about Uruk can be applied to the whole of Babylonia. We recognize a region organized into city-states with a society ordered according to hierarchical principles, a strictly organized economic and political administration, and formidable economic power, making Babylonia superior to all neighboring areas.

In other regions of the Near East, this dominance is expressed by numerous settlements that have left remains different from

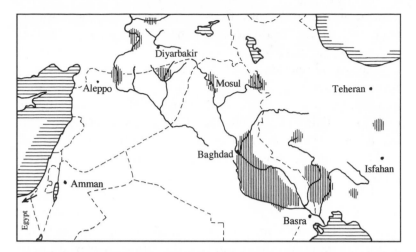

FIGURE 25. The spread of Uruk culture into neighboring regions

those of the local settlements, and that correspond to Babylonia in their architecture, pottery, and cylinder seals. At least a partial explanation may be that they were colonies or outposts (fig. 25). Settlements of this kind are found in Iran, Syria, and southeastern Anatolia and are probably connected with the procurement of raw materials. Their existence may suggest that Babylonia sometimes used its economic power to avoid paying fair price for the materials in question.

Babylonia's relation to the other early civilization in the area, that of ancient Egypt, was probably less dominant than influential. The Egyptians' partial adoption of the cylinder seal and the Babylonian influence on some forms of architecture in Egypt have no equivalent in Egyptian influence on Babylonia.

Since excavations in Uruk have barely touched levels earlier than 3200 BCE, we have to infer earlier forms from third- and fourth-millennium structures. Such inferences can safely be made mainly in economic matters, since these, more than other fields, have left tangible traces, which can be recovered by archaeology. Thus we can connect a number of finds to the genesis of writing, which itself belongs to the realm of economy.

The first extant written documents date from around 3200, at the end of the period that saw the emergence of structures already discussed. From the very earliest findings, writing appears as a fully developed system. With few exceptions, signs are stable, and both the use of script and the arrangement of the text on the tablet show no uncertainties. It has been suggested that this suddenness resulted from precursors that either have not yet been found or were written on materials unable to survive the Mesopotamian climate.

If, however, instead of looking for older forms of writing, we look for simpler methods of information storage, we uncover the prehistory of writing, from primitive methods of recording information to more complex systems, culminating in the writing system itself. Seals have been mentioned as an early medium of information storage (figs. 7 and 26a). Going back to the same period, the sixth millennium BCE, we know of small clay tokens with different geometric shapes standing for numbers or amounts (figs. 8 and 26b); unfortunately, there is no way of linking specific numbers to specific shapes. When tokens of this kind were combined with others and stored together, any number could be reproduced and recorded. Both seals and clay tokens, however, recorded only one piece of information: a person or a number.

For several millennia, both methods seem to have satisfied economic needs. Only after the middle of the fourth millennium did the situation change in Babylonia. The stamp seal was replaced by the cylinder seal, which was better equipped to provide a large and growing clientele with individual means of identificaton. In addition, the cylinder could be rolled over a clay lid in overlapping bands in order to imprint the entire surface and thus protect it. Thus personal protection via the authority of the seal owner was reinforced by an impersonal, mechanical protection, perhaps a function of the larger number of people taking part in economic matters. As before, however, this device allowed only one piece of information to be recorded (fig. 26d).

The use of clay tokens too was extended. Besides simple geometric shapes, the tokens could assume fairly complex forms, or even the shape of objects (fig. 26a), but again, they could represent only one piece of information. A further development did away with this limitation.

Not very long before the emergence of writing, hollow clay balls appeared, whose surface was covered entirely by seal impressions and

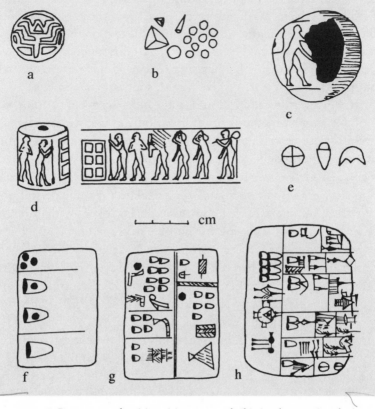

FIGURE 26. Precursors of writing: (a) stamp seal; (b) simple counting devices; (c) sealed bulla (hollow clay ball); (d) cylinder seal; (e) complex counters; (f) numerical tablet; (g) accounting tablet, ca. 3200 BCE; (h) accounting tablet, ca. 3000 BCE

which contained a number of different numerical tokens (fig. 26c). This marks a decisive step, for information on both a number and the person responsible could be recorded in the same medium. There was also a second method: on the surface of a flattened cake of clay, different indentations, standing for numbers, were made with a stylus. Subsequently, a cylinder seal would be rolled over the entire surface, so that information on both a number and a person were recorded (fig. 26f).

Both methods should be understood as answers to the economic demand for more complex means of control. At the moment when someone came up with the idea of a script that could widen the range of information to be stored, the script was recognized as an encompassing answer. To implement the system was just a matter of time.

All these advances took place only after the Ubaid period, pointing to an enormous acceleration of the process, especially after its stagnation for several thousand years. By consulting the results of the research on ancient climate and on the hinterland of Uruk, we can date this acceleration to the few centuries before 3200.

The inconsistent sedimentation of the layers forming the seabed of the Persian Gulf has been mentioned earlier. Most important was a relatively quick change during the fourth millennium from a humid climate to a cooler and dryer one, diminishing the amount of water in the rivers. Archaeological deep soundings have revealed remains of alluvial levels and reed in the lowest courses, suggesting humidity and an abundance of water during the period preceding the fourth millennium. These observations first led to an interpretation of the deposits as evidence of the flood described in the *Gilgamesh Epic* and the Old Testament, but they have since been shown to be local events only. The higher levels clearly indicated a normal occupation.

These results can usefully be linked to observations in the hinterland of Uruk. Objects found above any ancient settlement—mostly pottery sherds, which by their appearance can be attributed to a specific period—have enabled us to draw maps that include all settlements inhabited during a particular period. Two such maps pertain to phases between the end of the Ubaid and 3200: the map of the earlier phase, up to about 3500, shows eleven contemporary sites; that of the later phase shows 110 (fig. 27). Assuming that the climatic shift was felt by the middle of the fourth millennium, we could argue that occupation prior to 3500 was sparse because settlement was impeded by marshes and widespread, devastating floods. In the later phase, by contrast, the shift had caused the water to retreat and had rendered large parts of the country inhabitable.

The map of the later phase, between 3500 and 3200, illustrates a density of settlements and population hitherto unknown anywhere in the Near East. The problems we have discussed with regard

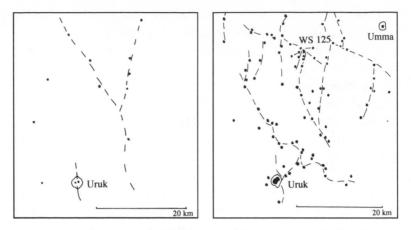

FIGURE 27. Settlements in the Uruk countryside, ca. 3600 BCE (left) and ca. 3200 BCE (right)

to earlier periods—those created by ever increasing populations living close to each other and the need for conflict management—are probably a mere shadow of the multiple and varied problems emerging at this point. All the new structures can now be explained as efforts to reduce and manage conflicts. No doubt, earlier experiences were made use of in this endeavor, for some of these new settlers probably came from areas that had already developed rules for societal containment.

The question of the ethnic affiliations of the population must be raised again here. In all probability, some of the immigrants responsible for the enormous increase in settlements came from the northern part of the Babylonian plain, where settlements were decreasing at the time. But the sheer quantity of immigrants suggests that other groups must have originated elsewhere. The Sumerians may have been one of these groups. This period probably saw the formation of the multiethnic society of Babylonia, which left continuing traces. That so far we have not been able to identify a particular language behind the earliest written documents may indicate that the script was deliberately retained in a form that could be used by all ethnic groups.

The period discussed in this chapter was decisive in setting the course for the future. A slight climatic shift rendered an inhospitable, humid area into an inviting, fertile region, mainly because enough water remained, temporarily, at least, for watering the fields. Basic experience in handling of societal and agricultural problems was readily available from the neighboring regions but was adjusted to new and greater needs. An extraordinarily mature urban society soon emerged. With its economic dominance, early Babylonian civilization exerted a manifold influence on neighboring regions.

For many centuries, Babylonia, or the southern part of Mesopotamia, was the driving force behind development in the ancient Near East.

4 City-States and the Way toward the Central State (Ca. 3200–2350 BCE)

With political and economic dominance over an extensive surrounding area, as well as a structured city government, the Babylonian cities of the late fourth millennium BCE met the criteria for
city-states. We have enough evidence to demonstrate that by the
first half of the third millennium, at the latest, major cities such
as Kish, Nippur, Isin, Lagash, Eridu, and Ur belong to the same
category as Uruk. To judge from the archaeological findings, all
Babylonia was a more or less homogeneous cultural unit, with
very few local variants. This uniformity is best illustrated by the
script, which in style and technique is so similar in all parts of the
country that we have to postulate close cooperation in the field of
scribal education.

The period immediately following 3000 BCE, known as Jemdet
Nasr after the place of its discovery, was largely a continuation of
Late Uruk. A change in the appearance of cylinder seals resulted
from the common trend to speed up and facilitate labor processes,
for we find that the traces of the cutting wheel were hardly ever
reworked (fig. 28). While time was saved in production, the seals
looked a little sketchy. Script developed continuously, and new ways
of organizing text on the tablet permitted greater complexity in
content. A new and speedier writing technique was introduced: the
lines in the signs were no longer incised but were dug with a stylus
held at a slant. In this way, the script began to attain the abstract
appearance of later cuneiform writing (figs. 26g–h and 29). In
pottery technology, mass production on the wheel was initiated. A
large lump of clay was put onto the wheel and formed into a cone,
only the top of which would be used for drawing out a bowl. After

FIGURE 28. Modern impression of a cylinder seal, ca. 3000 BCE. Traces of the grinding wheel are used for stylistic effect.

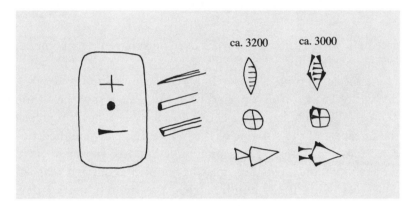

FIGURE 29. Shapes of styluses and their traces

a piece of the cone had been cut off and reshaped, a new bowl could be started immediately (fig. 30). The urge to speed up production, which we have already noted, continued in all areas.

In spite of this continuity, 3200 marks one radical change: the total reorganization of Uruk's major districts, primarily Eanna (fig. 31). Its footprint and surrounding wall remained the same, but instead of the many buildings of various sizes and styles, with no clear architectural center, a new central edifice appeared, almost certainly a temple, though only the terrace upon which it stood has survived. The terrace was surrounded by smaller buildings, which cannot have served the same functions as those of the preceding Late Uruk period. Only the minimal remains of a monumental

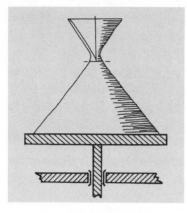

FIGURE 30. Potters wheel with lump of clay

gate indicate the presence of what once must have been an imposing complex.

At the same time, a marked change occurred in the western district of Uruk. After a period of decay, which saw the White Temple falling into ruins, the entire area took on a new character: the terrace and the remains of the White Temple were incorporated into a gigantic terrace, some three hundred thousand cubic meters in volume. This one must have taken about five years to construct, with fifteen hundred men working ten hours a day. A corresponding process was the architectural reorganization of Eanna, discussed above, with its central temple, like that of the former western central district, raised on a terrace. This change must have pertained to the political-administrative sector—the large meeting halls having disappeared—as well as to cultic life, for Eanna's new central temple on a terrace represented a concentration of religious power.

At the very end of the Late Uruk period we observe yet another change. Earlier, Babylonia had maintained such close ties to regions to its west, north, and east that they might be considered colonies or outposts. Evidence of these connections disappears almost completely, and very rapidly. Instead of a Uruk-centered network encompassing Mesopotamia and certain neighboring areas, during the Jemdet Nasr period we see the formation of local networks in those areas. The best known of these is the Proto-Elamite network, which connected Susiana (or Khuzestan) not with

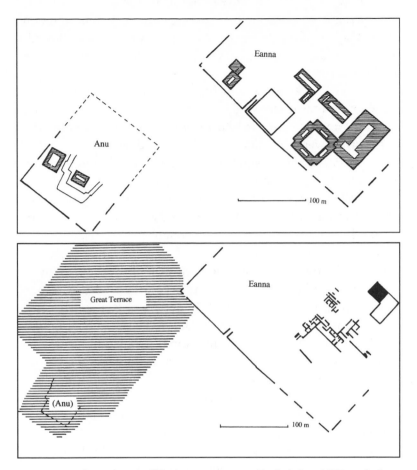

FIGURE 31. Central area of Uruk, ca. 3200 BCE (Archaic Level IV), and after the reorganization, ca. 3000 BCE (Archaic Level III)

Babylonia but with the inner-Iranian plateau, as far as Seistan to the east. The rearrangements in Uruk may have been a reaction to the dissolution of the Uruk network and the realignment of the political landscape.

The period following 3000 BCE is traditionally known as Early Dynastic, so named because records of the first dynasties of rulers during this period have been recovered. Though of unknown significance, an enigmatic new type of brick serves as a marker for the period. The new brick, no longer flat on all sides, was convex on top, like a cake baked in a rectangular pan. The reason for its strange shape is unclear. In conjunction with a different technique of bricklaying, these "plano-convex" bricks may have allowed a speedier building process than was possible with the smaller bricks used formerly.

The new bricks were used for one of the most monumental works in Uruk, the city wall, nine and one-half kilometers long, with nine hundred semicircular towers and several gates fortified by massive towers (see chap. 3, fig. 15). According to the *Gilgamesh Epic,* it was Gilgamesh who had this wall built. Although we have none of his original inscriptions, he is known as king of Uruk from the so-called Sumerian King List. The archaeological dating of the city wall to somewhere between 3000 and 2900 corresponds to the period during which Gilgamesh is thought to have reigned.

The city wall surrounded an area of more than five square kilometers, twice the size the city had been around 3200. Virtually the entire area within the confines of the city wall was settled, as were large sections outside of the wall. In other words: the urban area of Uruk had almost tripled in two hundred years, a development which cannot have resulted from normal population growth but must have been connected to changes in the hinterland.

After the 110 settlements of the Late Uruk period, far fewer remained, but these had increased in size. If we look at one little cluster to the northeast of Uruk, formerly consisting of eleven settlements grouped around a central one, we see that by 2900 only three of the small ones remained, while the central settlement had grown several times as large as its original size (fig. 32). By a parallel process, other formerly middle-range settlements had now attained the size of cities.

Instead of the tangled system of rivers and streams of the Late Uruk period, attesting to the ubiquitous presence of irrigation water, the number of watercourses decreased, their new, straight alignment indicating their transformation into canals. This marks the beginning of what later became the hallmark of Babylonia: large-scale canal and irrigation systems.

By 3000 at the latest, the decrease in water had become a problem; what once had made possible the comprehensive settlement of the Babylonian plain started to be in short supply. Patches of land increasingly were left without direct access to naturally flowing

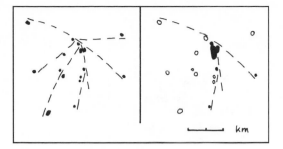

FIGURE 32. Group of settlements northeast of Uruk, ca. 3200 and 2900 BCE. Open circles indicate settlements abandoned by 2900 BCE.

water. Wherever possible, water was brought into those areas by means of long canals, but numerous settlements had to be abandoned. Their populations appear to have moved into the main settlements, causing the rapid growth of the latter; Uruk's enormous increase in size is an obvious example of this trend.

By the middle of the third millennium, most of the Babylonian population lived in cities. We can plausibly assume that considerable efforts had to be invested in the control of conflicts, to which city dwellers were ever more susceptible, and in other problems such as the provisioning of the urban population.

The forced introduction of canal irrigation turned the continuous agricultural area of Babylonia into a system of "irrigation oases," each fed by a main canal that in turn was fed by the Euphrates. The fate of such oases depended on securing the necessary influx of water—increasingly problematic in light of the drying climate and the rising competition for water.

Dependence on canal irrigation had yet another consequence. Since the amount of water in the rivers fluctuated considerably from one year to the next, the supply of water was unreliable. Areas both small and large at the margins of such systems could not count on receiving sufficient water every year. In response, a way of life that we might call semisedentary developed in those marginal areas: in bad years, more emphasis was put on herding. The presence of these inner-Babylonian semisedentary or seminomadic groups had long-term consequences: it facilitated the infiltration of groups from outside with a similar organization of life.

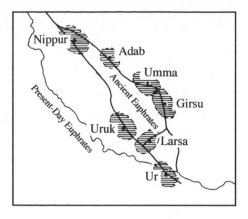

FIGURE 33. Babylonian
cities with their probable
terrains or areas of influence,
ca. 2700 BCE

In order to provide enough food for the urban population, the
settlements that only recently had attained the status of city had to
enlarge their terrain. Probably in more cases than one—though only
one has been documented—these new areas of influence touched
or even overlapped the terrains of older cities, creating conflicts of
a new kind (fig. 33). To be sure, even before cities and city-states
began to compete with each other, such conflicts may have led to
military operations. A number of ancient literaryworks, including
those concerning King Gilgamesh, refer to military events in the
early periods. The assumption that conflicts were always possible
is further supported by the existence of city walls. But now the
loss of safe distances between neighboring cities created conflicts
inherent in the system and therefore difficult to resolve.

We know more about these later clashes because the recording
of historical information changed dramatically around 2600 BCE.
For nearly seven hundred years, writing had been used almost
exclusively to record economic data. From the middle of the third
millennium, however, inscriptions have emerged that describe the
deeds of rulers and their family background. For the first time we
are in a position to name individual kings and whole dynasties,
and to envisage the historical context. The appearance of these
first detailed texts coincided with no specific political event, and
the actions related were no more important than those of earlier
times. But now they were recorded in writing.

Border quarrels between neighboring cities are attested to in royal inscriptions from the city of Lagash from around 2500 BCE. They describe an ongoing conflict, lasting several generations, with the city of Umma over a region and a canal at their common border. Various attempts to find a solution are described, including war, a treaty, or the use of an arbitrator, but in the next generation the conflict flared up again, seemingly intractable. Only by abandoning the organizational system of the city-state could a solution be found: when larger territories, or states, were formed, intercity conflicts could be handled as intrastate matters.

Although we are still unable to make authoritative pronouncements about religious belief during this period, there are hints as to cultic organization. The reorganization of Uruk's central area with the terrace and raised temple furnished both this area and the entire city with a clear cultic focus. This manifestation of the basic ideology that every city should have a specific deity attached remained the characteristic feature of Babylonian cities. The earliest written documents use the same sign for the names of the city and of the respective deity. To what degree the equation influenced the organization of the city is an open question. All we can say is that no evidence has been found of cult personnel among the leading figures in the list of titles. The sources are unclear. On the one hand, the ruler is unquestionably seen as the highest-ranking servant of the deity of his city, as expressed occasionally in royal inscriptions. On the other hand, the existence of particular buildings that serve neither cultic nor residential purposes and are hence identified as palaces, as well as sources that mention apparent violations of priestly privileges on the part of rulers, point to a growing emancipation of the ruler. The challenges of political leadership along with the ruler's ambiguous relations to religious authority led to a new definition of the status of ruler. In the light of subsequent history, what we see here probably marks the beginning of strained relations between temple and palace.

Besides the official cult of the city deity, which primarily involved the ruler, we find in each city a varying number of temples devoted to the worship of other major gods. Unfortunately, we have no idea why cultic buildings and shrines differed from each other. Did they have different clienteles, or did they respond to different needs of the worshipers? It seems likely that the temples

FIGURE 34. Male statue (height: 72 cm) and female statue (height: 59 cm) from Eshnunna, ca. 2700 BCE

formed part of the official cult, in contrast to findings that may be interpreted as signs of personal piety. In shrines integrated into normal residential districts, limestone statues, mostly of males, were found in walled chambers (fig. 34). They are reminiscent of the custom, known from later texts, of placing statues in temples, where they were supposed to represent the donor and to ask the deity to grant the donor a long life. Once in a while these statues seem to have been removed and ritually buried. Their apparent purpose was to create a personal relation between donor and deity; the donor hoping for the deity's protection. The deities that were worshiped and prayed to in this manner were not the major gods but local, lower-level deities. A distinction between official cult and personal piety is also attested to by the rulers of the city-state of Lagash, who in their inscriptions always emphasized that they received their orders from their (city-)god Ningirsu, while making it clear that they considered Shul-Utul to be their personal, tutelary god.

The development of Early Dynastic art—except for the decoration on the cylinder seals—is difficult to assess. The art of the Late Uruk period, and probably that of Jemdet Nasr, had served primarily to glorify the ruler. It was official art, unlike the Early

FIGURE 35. One side of the "Stela of Vultures" of Eannatum of Lagash, ca. 2450 BCE

Dynastic statues that we described as unofficial art. The seals and the statues clearly belonged to different spheres and served different functions and thus should not be used for tracing the general development of art. While the majority of the prayer statues exhibit an abstract-geometric style, the older pieces are more naturalistic. Since we have no examples of official art from the same period as the prayer statues, we cannot determine whether their differences attest to a change of style over time or merely express the contrast between official and unofficial art.

In the later part of Early Dynastic period, official art was represented primarily by reliefs depicting specific events, such as the "Stela of the Vultures," commemorating the victory of Eannatum of Lagash over the neighboring city of Umma (fig. 35). There are certain governing principles. Representations of the body do not attempt to render natural features; details of a face, of a body, or of an entire composition are put together according to a predetermined value system. What is important is larger than what is unimportant; for example, eyes are disproportionately large, and persons of authority are taller than subordinates. A specific figure may be identified by an accompanying inscription, though no physical likeness is intended, as exemplified by the seated figure of Dudu, the scribe (fig. 36).

Deities are rarely represented, but when they are, they are depicted as even taller than the ruler. A niche in the rear wall of the inner sanctum of temples of this period suggests that it was

FIGURE 36. Statue of the scribe Dudu, ca. 2500 BCE (height: 45 cm).

once occupied by the statue of a deity, but we have found no examples.

One or two generations before the appearance of fully legible texts, the world of deities had been systematized in a list of their names that was excavated in the city of Shuruppak. The order of the main gods—An, Enlil, Inanna, Enki, Nanna, and Utu—so closely resembles later constructions of hierarchical and family relations among the gods that we suspect even the early order to have been constructed theologically. It is unclear whether the deities were listed in their capacity as gods of the major cities, or whether they had already been incorporated into a genealogical system with specific categories, such as the goddess of love and war or the gods of water, moon, and sun. The list includes more than five hundred names, many of which are otherwise unknown. Only rarely can we identify the deity worshiped in the various temples, and only by taking for granted a continuous cultic tradition can we use later sources to reconstruct the affinity between certain cities and specific deities. At a time when more detailed texts that might have helped us were being written, systematizations had already supplanted earlier thinking with respect to the gods.

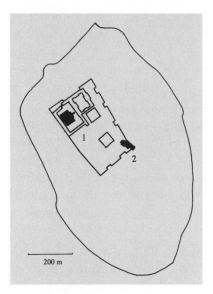

FIGURE 37. City of Ur with the central temple area (1) and the royal cemetery (2)

A different approach to religious conceptions is offered by burials, known in particular from the city of Ur, whose origins go back to the fifth millennium. Later, Ur is known to have been the cult center of the moon god Nanna. During the late part of the Early Dynastic period, the central area, the seat of the local leadership as well as of the central cultic installations, was considerably higher than its immediate surroundings, with a sharp drop separating it from the urban area (fig. 37). Between 2600 and 2000 BCE the southeastern slope was used as a burial ground. At the same time it served as a dump for all the rubble and refuse from the central area. Graves were dug into the rubble but were also overlaid by new material within the same period. The dead were accompanied by an abundance of burial objects such as jewelry, weapons, tools, and pottery vessels; the kinds of vessels indicate that the dead were given both solid and liquid provisions for the journey to the underworld. The living must have held firm concepts both of a life after death and of the rituals the family had to perform in order to ease the existence of the dead. These included continuous offerings of liquid and solid foods, which required that the burial site had to be marked—at least for some time. Remains of buildings or chapels at burial sites have been found only in connection with the elaborate tombs to be discussed below. Reflections of the concepts of a life after death are found in the poem *Inanna's Descent to the Underworld,* one of the writings that uses myth in an attempt to explain the seasonal withering of vegetation: to gain her own release from the underworld, Inanna sends Dumuzi, the god of vegetation, as her substitute, thus causing vegetation to die off.

When the cemetery at Ur was first begun, seventeen funerary complexes were erected, most of them with walled tombs. These are known as Royal Tombs of Ur, though only a few bear inscriptions indicating that rulers or members of their families had been buried there. But the fabulous richness of these tombs certainly supports the designation. In many of the complexes, a large number of human burial gifts have been found, lying in a kind of forecourt. An entire household may have been buried in such a complex—high-ranking personnel, male and female personal servants, musicians and soldiers, as well as wagons complete with draft animals and drivers. Some of the musicians still had their fingers on the cords of lyres fashioned out of precious material. The orderly and peaceful position of the corpses suggests that they took poison. These servants were supposed to ensure the deceased an adequate life in the underworld. Since these tombs go back to the period before detailed texts appeared, we cannot hope to find reference to them in original sources. Such funerary customs were apparently abandoned soon afterward, for there is no help from later texts either.

The rich burial gifts are a clear case of conspicuous consumption, an excessive show of wealth with the aim of increasing the prestige of the deceased. The human burial gifts too may be seen as part of this excess (fig. 38). The elaborate furnishings attest to a general wealth associated mainly with the Royal Tombs but to a lesser degree with private tombs as well, which in some cases contained numerous vessels, jewelry made of precious metals and stones, and tools and weapons made of copper or bronze.

In almost one-quarter of the 1,850 tombs, both royal and private, that have been excavated, cylinder seals were found. As mentioned earlier, seals were a prerequisite for anyone who took part in economic life, and in order to identify an owner, every seal had to bear an individual design. Decorations on seals therefore had to

FIGURE 38. Artist's representation of part of the burial ceremony, with human sacrifices before their death, at one of the Royal Tombs of Ur, ca. 2550 BCE

FIGURE 39. Headdress of Queen Puabi, found in her tomb at Ur, ca. 2550 BCE

vary widely. By the middle of the third millennium, when pictorial variability appeared insufficient to guarantee identification, the owner's name in writing was added to the seal pattern—another innovation.

In general, cylinder seals are an important source of information, for their role in economic life made them ubiquitous. Unlike statues or reliefs—rare in some periods, nonexistent in others—cylinder seals, as miniature art offering an abundance of illustrative

FIGURE 40. Modern impressions of seals with the most common motifs of the late Early Dynastic period: animal contest and symposium, ca. 2550 BCE

material, lend themselves to studying the development of artistic expression over long periods.

It would be natural to assume that variability was achieved by enlisting as many topics as possible from the world of intellectual and religious concepts. Contrary to our expectation, however, relatively few topics served as the basic reservoir, but these were rendered in great variety. The favorite theme of the Early Dynastic was a fight between wild and domestic animals, the latter sometimes supported by human figures. The lion and the bull were basic elements. Some compositions seem elaborate to the point of fussiness; for example, human and animal figures in an upright position are arranged as if in a braid, criss-crossing each other (fig. 40, upper image).

One protective figure is the bull-man, human above, bull below. Though this enigmatic figure remains alive throughout Mesopotamian art, neither his name nor his function has been identified. He is probably one of the many demons known from later periods. We are equally ignorant about the general theme of animal contest.

Since only a limited number of extant seals bear personal inscriptions, it is difficult to establish a possible relation between the material and decoration of a seal and the social status of its owner. But one theme indicates status: the so-called symposium, or drinking scene (fig. 40, lower image). Two or more persons sit facing each other, either drinking from cups or sucking some liquid from a large vessel through drinking tubes—it was probably beer, which according to written sources was produced in great quantities. The seated figures are attended by servants. The scene may be expanded by additional figures, dancing or playing music. A second register may contain different scenes, such as an animal contest. Seals with a symposium as their main theme are usually made of lapis lazuli. Most of these were found in the Royal Tombs of Ur.

A description of this period would be incomplete without reference to Babylonia's connections to its neighboring regions, primarily the long-distance trade relations that can be inferred from the diverse materials as found in the Royal Tombs of Ur. Nothing is known about the provenance of gold. Silver and most of the semiprecious colored stones, however, come from the high ranges of the Zagros to the east. An even greater distance had to be covered to secure lapis lazuli, as this stone is mined only in Badakhshan, the northeasternmost corner of present-day Afghanistan. Of particular interest are beads of reddish-brown carnelian with white lines etched on their surface. Since this etching technique originated in the Indus valley, these beads are the earliest evidence of direct contacts between urban civilization in that area and Mesopotamian high culture.

Archaeological finds have also revealed ties to the region of present-day Syria and southeastern Anatolia. By the middle of the third millennium, city-states in the Syrian region had apparently reached such a level of complexity that the Babylonian cuneiform script was adopted in the belief that it could help to control their problems. Thousands of cuneiform texts have been found in the West Syrian city of Ebla and some in other places as well. This adoption proved to have unforeseen repercussions on the culture of Babylonia.

Until that time, cuneiform was used primarily to record economic data. The spoken language did not need to be rendered, as catchwords were sufficient. In limited instances, signs were used in a manner that denoted their phonetic value but not their primary meaning. Since Sumerian is by and large a monosyllabic language, it could be represented by stringing together the appropriate word signs. But that had to change when Semitic groups living both in Babylonia and in Syrian cities started using cuneiform to represent their own language. Unlike Sumerian, which indicates person and tense in verb forms by attaching the appropriate particles to the stem of the word, the inflecting Semitic languages modify the stem. For this purpose, signs have to be stripped of their original meaning and used phonetically. Although inherent in the writing system from the beginning, this function was hardly ever used. When speakers of Semitic languages used it more freely, Sumerian speakers must have realized that this extended use of the signs would serve well in writing their own language. With the new technique, all parts of Sumerian language could be expressed in writing. From then on, spoken language could be rendered in detail, allowing Sumerian literary, historical, and religious texts to be written. Thus, with the help of a neighboring region, Babylonian culture availed itself of the ability to put in writing the host of texts that so far had been transmitted orally—not to mention the subsequent development of a high literary culture.

The middle of the third millennium also offered the possibility of testing new political structures. The permanent conflict between Lagash and Umma had shown why cities unintentionally got involved in unending conflicts. Among attempts to find solutions, the one used most frequently was the formation of larger territories by conquering neighboring cities. This policy may have been driven by personal ambition and striving for power, but it did offer an answer to urgent problems. These attempts all ended with the close of the conqueror's reign, or sooner. But they paved the way for the first unification of Babylonia under Sargon, the founder of the dynasty of Akkad, which lasted for four generations.

5 The First Central States (Ca. 2350–1595 BCE)

Why did rulers of Babylonian cities in the middle of the third millennium try to incorporate other city-states into their territory by conquest instead just raiding them as was customary before? Was it just an expression of their personal desire for more power, or was it something more, a strategy in pursuit of higher goals? At the very least, the idea of creating a larger territory must have been attractive enough to find followers. After early attempts had failed, measures were conceived to ensure success. The trend for the following centuries can be summarized as transferring partial sovereignty from the cities to the capital of a central state.

The slow but continuing consolidation of the central state that took place between the Akkad dynasty and the Third Ur dynasty obscures the fact that this form of government did not meet with universal approval. It was even abandoned several times, with full power restored to the city-states. This back-and-forth stopped when Babylonia became integrated into the political context of the larger Near East. At the beginning of the sixteenth century, the Hittite ruler Murshili inflicted the final blow on the ailing First Dynasty of Babylon by means of a blitz attack. After this shock, the old system no longer worked. The principle of city-states had had its day. Within the wider area of the Near East, territorial states were about to form, which would have given no chance of survival to a Babylonia fragmented into city-states.

It would be easy to explain these changes as a clash between the central ruler's striving for power on the one hand, and, on the other, the city lords' refusal to submit to a superimposed power. The matter should be looked at from a different angle, however.

At the end of the Early Dynastic period, Lugalzagesi, the local ruler of Umma, had conquered a substantial part of southern Babylonia, apparently using methods that were frowned on. Urukagina, the last ruler of Lagash, complained that Lugalzagesi committed the sin of destroying local temples. It speaks for the strong equation of city and city-god that Urukagina did not lay blame for this sin on Lugalzagesi personally but on the goddess of Umma. In still another perspective, Lugalzagesi's actions might not be thought sacrilegious but should be considered in the context of one of Babylonia's basic problems, which was to dominate the following centuries. Here we must take a brief look back.

In light of the increasing shortage of water for irrigation, it probably appeared advantageous to have a central authority for allocating this precious resource. But there was a fundamental argument against centralization. With the progressive division of Babylonia into irrigation oases, it was in the local interest that distribution of water within a locality should remain under local jurisdiction. Along with many reasons for a city's autonomy, notably the value of independence itself as worthy of protection, full control over the local irrigation system may have been the most viable argument of the city-states against a central state.

One institution was particularly susceptible to a city's potential loss of autonomy: the city deity, represented by the central temple and its priesthood. According to the ideology that prevailed during the late Early Dynastic, the local ruler was supposed to be merely the worldly representative of the city god. The rivalry therefore was not between local rulers and the central ruler but between city gods and the central ruler. Since the temples were the main seats of opposition, it was logical for Lugalzagesi to have them destroyed.

The defeat of Lugalzagesi, as well as the conquest of Uruk and Ur, made Sargon, who already controlled northern Babylonia, overlord over the south too. Although Sargon's origins remain obscure, he was said, like Moses, to have been found in a basket floating down the Euphrates and raised at the royal court. Later he served as cup-bearer for the king of the city of Kish in northern Babylonia, before starting his political career from the city of Akkad, from which we derive the name for both the language and the members of Babylonia's Semitic population. Akkad probably lay in the vicinity of Kish, though its location has not yet been identified. Like his former lord and probably the majority of the population of northern Babylonia, Sargon belonged to the Semitic sector. As other usurpers have done, he gave himself an official throne name: *sharru kenu,* Akkadian for "legitimate king," which in the Old Testament was transformed to "Sargon."

According to certain texts, Sargon was of a mature age when he ascended to the throne. In his earlier years he had likely seen at least one attempt to unite the country and had learned from its failure. In his own persuit of centralization, he ordered the trading ships from the Gulf of Persia and the Indus region (Meluhha, Magan, and Dilmun) to moor at the quay of his city of Akkad; the natural harbors of Ur and Lagash must have lost part of their income. A tightening political coherence is indicated by the statement that "sons of Akkad held the *ensi* offices in the country" (*ensi* was originally the title of local rulers, then of governors), meaning that Sargon's own people were put in charge of the conquered cities. Sargon even interfered with the local cults, as shown by the investiture of his daughter Enheduana as high priestess of Ur's city god Nanna. The formation of a standing task force may be inferred from the sentence that "fifty-four hundred men ate their bread in the presence of Sargon." In other words, important innovations, which helped the central state to survive for several generations, clearly originated with Sargon.

While Sumerian royal names were ceding to Akkadian (i.e. Semitic) names, the language of official inscriptions also changed. Granted, some Semitic names are known from the preceding period, such as like Mesalim, the ruler prior to Urnanshe who had arbitrated the dispute between Lagash and Umma around 2550 BCE, or Queen Puabi, who around that time was buried in one of the Royal Tombs of Ur. Likewise, some scribes of contemporary texts written in Sumerian bore Semitic names. So there is considerable evidence that members of the Akkadian population occupied important positions even before the time of Sargon.

Without a doubt, the language change encountered at this point was politically motivated. It is all the more surprising that, despite intense research, we have found no overt references to major or minor tensions or conflicts between Sumerians and Akkadians. Such

FIGURE 41. Fragment of one of Sargon's victory stelae, showing prisoners in line, ca. 2350 BCE (height: 21 cm)

tensions, if they existed, may have been partly obscured because the language of a name did not necessarily point to someone's ethnic affiliation. The name of Sargon's daughter Enheduana is Sumerian, whereas rulers of the Third Dynasty of Ur, which reintroduced Sumerian as the official language as part of its political program, have Semitic names like Shusin or Ibbisin.

More striking than the change in language was a fundamental change in artistic expression that occurred at the same time. Whether we look at reliefs, royal statuary, or cylinder seals, the differences are conspicuous, most notably the naturalistic rendering of bodily features (fig. 41). Natural representations of muscles and other details are in total contrast to the blocklike, out-of-proportion figures of the Early Dynastic period. The impression of freely acting, individual figures—both human and animal—is achieved by emphasizing contours, a technique that makes figures on both reliefs and seals stand out from the background. Whereas there was always an aversion to leaving part of the background blank, the background was now actually incorporated into the composition.

The commonest theme of the seals of the Early Dynastic period, the animal contest, remained dominant (fig. 42a), but the repertory was tremendously broadened. The new themes belonged mostly to the genre of mythological scenes (fig. 42c), including the interesting representation of a fight among gods. These scenes center mainly on deities and demons. Unfortunately we have not been able to

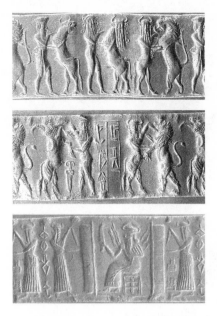

FIGURE 42. Modern impressions of seals of the Akkadian period, 2350–2150 BCE: animal contest; two pairs of contestants flanking a framed inscription; the sun god between doors opened by two demons.

identify the scenes, presumably based on then-popular myths, with any of the many myths known to us from literature.

In chapter 4 we mentioned a specific theme and kind of stone that revealed the social status of the seal owner. Among the seals of the Akkadian period, one group can be distinguished by the arrangement of the figures in an animal contest: in a heraldic manner, two pairs of fighting figures stand on either side of a framed inscription (fig. 42b). The unusually frequent inscriptions—which often add the family status and profession to the name—tell us that a large proportion of this group of seals belonged to members of the royal family or to high officials. Although we lack examples, it seems likely that other themes were similarly tied to social groups or professions.

The same change in style can be perceived on statues and reliefs. It is well illustrated by a comparison of the late Early Dynastic statue of Dudu (see chap. 4, fig. 36) with that of a man from Assur of the Akkadian period (fig. 43), or the "Stela of the Vultures" of Eannatum of Lagash (see chap. 4, fig. 35) with the fragment of one of Sargon's victory stelae (fig. 41). Everywhere we encounter a new fidelity to nature and to proportions.

FIGURE 43. Torso of a statue of a bearded man of the Akkadian period, from Assur, ca. 2300 BCE (height: 137 cm)

Totally outside the framework not only of Akkadian but also of ancient Near Eastern art is the victory stela of Naramsin (fig. 44). King Naramsin, who stands out because of his exceptional size, is seen in front of a high mountain and below three stars representing the divine support. His horned crown and an inscription show him as deified. According to the inscription, the event depicted is the victory of Naramsin and his army over the Lullubi, a group from the eastern mountains. Naramsin is facing the leader of the hostile forces of the Lullubi, who is depicted on a much smaller scale, begging for mercy while turning his feet in readiness to flee. Between these main characters an enemy soldier falls backward, struck by a spear.

Both armies are represented by individual figures. The victorious Akkadian army is more numerous and consists of officers bearing military standards and common soldiers bearing various weapons. Of the enemy forces, only three figures are shown close to the right margin; their spears are broken, and like their leader they are begging for mercy, while turning their feet to flee.

What is exceptional about this stela is the way the enemies' supplication to Naramsin has been transposed pictorially. The typical gesture is shown by the figure in front of the king, who

FIGURE 44. Victory stela of Naramsin of Akkad, ca. 2250 BCE (preserved height: 200 cm)

holds his right hand in front of his mouth while looking at the king. Normally this gesture would be repeated for the enemy figures, regardless of their position. Here, however, the essence of the gesture rather than the pictorial convention is retained: each enemy figure tilts his head and extends hand and arm so as to maintain one line from his mouth and hand to the face of the king; the lower he is located on the stela, the more he must tilt back his head and the higher he must extend his hand. This pictorial composition, with reciprocal parts, is otherwise unknown, and distinguishes the stela from all other works of ancient Near Eastern art.

As mentioned, Naramsin's horned crown depicts him as a god. This stela attests to a phenomenon frequent in later periods, both in the ancient Near East and elsewhere, but occurring here for the first time: the deification of rulers during their lifetime. Contemporary texts tell us that Naramsin was deified as a gift from the gods and as a reward for military successes. But this ruler was also believed to have deified himself, an act of hubris that contributed to Naramsin's bad image in later literary tradition. There may, however, be yet another explanation. Not only does Naramsin call himself "God of [the city of] Akkad," but also his subordinates address him this way in declarations of loyalty. Presumably this custom was part of an ideology that assigned a dominant role to the city deity, not only in political life but also in economic matters, based on the main temple's control of vast estates around the city. With his self-appointment as god of his city, Naramsin laid claim to those estates both in his own interest and to deprive his adversaries of their economic base.

This move was rightfully perceived as a general attack on the status of the priests. In a tendentious piece of literature, we read that Enlil, the father of the gods, intervenes in order to punish Naramsin: he calls upon the Guti—a group from the Eastern mountains like the Lullubi of the victory stela—to enter the country and to destroy the city of Akkad. Titled *The Curse of Akkad,* the story ends with Ishtar, the true goddess of Akkad and thus the figure mainly affected, rejoicing over the destruction of her city. The biased nature of the piece becomes evident in the assertion that Enlil was avenging the destruction of his temple in Nippur by Naramsin, whereas archaeological investigation has uncovered no traces of destruction but, on the contrary, has found evidence of restoration work carried out by Naramsin.

This story was probably written 150 years later, when Shulgi, the second king of the Third Dynasty of Ur, was to be warned against revealing too much arrogance. It perfectly exemplifies the tendentious character of much of the contemporary writing, including the Sumerian King List, which nevertheless serves as the main source for names, sequence, and length of regime of rulers and dynasties in the second half of the third millennium. Consciously distorting reality, the list suggests that the dynasties in the late Early Dynastic ruled one after the other, implying that Babylonia always has been ruled by one dynasty at a time. From a large number of original royal inscriptions, however, we know that several of these kings in fact ruled simultaneously in different cities. Another misrepresentation is the omission of the local rulers of the city-state of Lagash—an ironic gap since almost all written sources for the late Early Dynastic come from the capital, Girsu.

Aside from political writings of this kind, a wealth of literature was produced, some by a woman: Enheduana, Sargon's daughter and the high priestess of Nanna in Ur, is credited with the composition of two long hymns to the goddess Inanna/Ishtar in addition to an entire collection of temple hymns.

Because of the ever-growing opposition to central rule, every member of the Akkadian dynasty had to spend the first years of his reign fighting off various coalitions of Babylonian cities and regaining central control over them. During Naramsin's reign, it is quite possible that a general uprising threatened to dissolve the central state. Although the reasons for this turbulence remain unclear—apart from the cities' constant striving for independence—the consequences are plain. The last member of the Sargon family, optimistically named Sharkalisharri, "King of all Kings," apparently ended his reign with little more than his own city and some countryside. In this poorly documented period, other parts of the former Akkadian empire, such as Uruk and Lagash, were already ruled by local dynasties.

The assertion in *The Curse of Akkad* that groups from the eastern mountains overthrew the Akkadian state is certainly exaggerated. It is true, however, that these groups from the eastern mountains, whom we have met before under the names of Guti or Lullubi, on the one hand created widespread unrest by their raids, and on the other hand managed to establish a foothold on the eastern fringe of the Babylonian plain, where they set up a regime of their own, the rulers of which are called "kings" in the Sumerian King List.

The cities' newly won independence was short-lived, but it did live long enough, according to our sources, for the cities to resume their former organization and relationships with no difficulty. Having retained their basic structures under the umbrella of the central state, cities were capable of taking charge as soon as the central state ailed. All of our relevant documents come from Girsu, the only surviving city in the former state of Lagash, and all pertain to the local ruler, Gudea. Numerous inscribed statues (fig. 45), two long hymns for the building of the main temple, and thousands of cuneiform texts present a picture decidedly different from that of the preceding period. A deliberate reference to pre-Sargonic times is apparent not only in the reintroduction of the Sumerian language but at all levels of public life. This period, it seems, was making

FIGURE 45. Seated statue of Gudea of Lagash, ca. 2120 BCE (height: 45 cm)

almost excessive attempts to recreate former conditions. Inscriptions concerning Gudea, for instance, report only pious deeds—the erection of temples and care for the gods—in accordance with a basic concept of the ruler as merely a regent for the city god Ningirsu. A similar attitude, if less overt, is found in the inscriptions relating to the last pre-Sargonic ruler of Lagash. The numerous statues of Gudea evidence a peculiar mixture of direct continuity and adaptation to pre-Sargonic principles. While the representation of parts of the human body—chest, hands, fingers, and upper arms, with the articulation of muscles and other details—hardly differs from the Akkadian tradition, the body's general proportions are totally ignored, as in the late Early Dynastic.

Since the inscriptions focus only on Gudea's pious deeds, we get no feeling for major political changes in the period. It must have been at this time that the Guti were finally expelled from Babylonia by a coalition of several cities, led by Utuhegal, a ruler of Uruk. Since the final battle apparently took place not too far west of Umma, the city of Girsu may have formed part of the coalition. Also at this time, Babylonia was reunited by Urnamma, a brother of Utuhegal's and also one of his generals, who took advantage of his brother's victory by setting up his own regime in Ur. The only general information we gain from Gudea's records is that neither

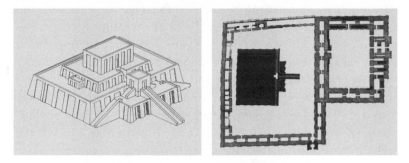

FIGURE 46. Ziqqurrat of Ur (H. Schmid's suggested reconstruction) and plan of the complex, ca. 2100 BCE

the Guti nor other factors disturbed the long-distance trade: for the construction and decoration of the temple of Ningirsu, Gudea obtained material from afar, including timber from the Indus area and cedar beams from Lebanon.

Unification under Urnamma must have come swiftly and without major difficulties. While firming up the administrative apparatus—for instance, by defining administrative districts with fixed boundaries—he took measures to avoid former mistakes. Among such measures was a master plan for reorganizing the central temple areas according to a consistent design. In each case the center was to be occupied by a *ziqqurrat:* a high terrace consisting of two superimposed huge rectangular platforms built of mud bricks, forming a base for the temple (fig. 46). This architecture recalls the earlier type of temple on a terrace but has an impressive new solution for access: a flight of steps leading up to the midpoint of one side, with two subsidiary flights, opposite each other and perpendicular to the first. Monumental edifices of this sort, surrounded by administration buildings and courtyards, are known to have existed in Ur and Uruk, as well as other cities, as evidenced by surviving fragments or written references.

Because of their size and location in the city center, these buildings unmistakably symbolized the power of the central ruler. At the same time, however, they emphasized the grandeur of the local city deity, whose former, presumably smaller temples had given way to the new monuments. Urnamma's architectural program was part of a political strategy that responded to history. This ruler certainly had extensive information on the dynasty of Akkad, and he himself must have witnessed the final dissolution of the Akkadian empire. He was no doubt aware that the main opposition to central rule originated with the local priesthoods. Urnamma's measures, with their grandiose and visible enhancement of local prestige, took the wind out of his opponent's sails more effectively than did Naramsin's frontal attack. Nonetheless, it was obvious where the real power lay. That next to no protest arose from the priesthoods confirms the wisdom of Urnamma's course.

The most momentous undertaking in the reign of Urnamma's son and successor Shulgi was a reform of the administration. The twenty-second year of Shulgi's reign saw the beginning of an unprecedented flood of written material concerned with practical matters rather than literary themes. An element of the reform seems to have been the extension of what had to be recorded in writing as well as the standardization of forms for documents. The fact that Shulgi himself boasts of having founded two schools adds the necessary piece to the mosaic. To exercise better control of the economy, the number of scribes who graduated from the training schools was drastically increased, the script was simplified, and the forms were standardized. Once the scribes had memorized these standardized forms, they could complete them by merely inserting the relevant data, which must have speeded things up. The training programs may even have been split between those who were to end up as scribes in an agricultural establishment or a storehouse on the one hand, and those destined to become highly specialized authors of literary compositions or royal hymns on the other. The appearance of the new genre of royal hymns, or court poetry, suggests that the schools founded by Shulgi may have been located in the palace.

Because of the reform of scribal education, the Ur III period ended up as one of the most literate times in ancient Near Eastern history. We need only look at the seals. Instead of the wide variety of themes used for identification in the Early Dynastic, the Ur III period hardly ever used more than one: the so-called introduction or presentation scene (fig. 47). A supplicant stands in front of a king or a god; in the latter case, he is often presented by a servant deity. Along with this pictorial limitation, the quantity of

FIGURE 47. Modern impression of a seal from the Ur III period with presentation scene and inscription, ca. 2100 BCE

inscribed seals rose massively. Apparently the inscription alone could now be trusted to identify the seal owner. Quite frequently, only the inscribed part was stamped on the clay surface instead of the entire seal.

The total control of the economy aimed primarily at answering the problems of the constantly deteriorating the water situation. Whereas the availability of water had originally enabled the large-scale settling of the Babylonian plain, its continuing decrease had prompted the construction of canal systems. From the middle of the third millennium on, however, frequent new ways had to be conceived to keep water available, hence the introduction of weirs, locks, and retaining pools. Increasingly, water was used solely for irrigation, leaving none for drainage. Because of the high temperatures in the region and the correspondingly high evaporation, the freshwater grew saltier. Irrigation, therefore, further increased the amount of salt that had already accumulated in the fields, thanks to the groundwater. Since drainage was neglected, these accumulated salts were no longer carried off, resulting in large patches of barren land. Though we do not know precisely when this problem became critical, agricultural texts from the Ur III period characterize fields in the vicinity of Ur as "located at brackish water," "with heaps of salt," in a "salty place," or on "salty soil," in order to explain their low yields.

Thus, in addition to the lessening of irrigation water, the agricultural area was limited by the increase in salinization. As the population grew, so did the need for food, and by the end of the third millennium the situation must have been alarming. Two solutions were possible: intensifying cultivation, which was chancy at a time when fertilization was unknown, or intensifying controls in order to prevent goods disappearing into unauthorized channels.

The at least superficial reconciliation of temple and palace, the creation of administrative districts headed by officers who could be transferred elsewhere, and the general tightening of the administrative apparatus under the Third Dynasty of Ur had established a state which, although the districts still enjoyed a certain autonomy, was far more centralized than anything that had gone before. The preconditions for a long survival had been met. That the regime was cut short from without rather than from within is therefore not surprising.

Sharkalisharri, the last Akkadian king, had already been forced to fight off invaders who, under the collective name of Amorites, had by the time of the Third Dynasty of Ur grown to be the menace that brought the empire to its collapse. A wall built by Shulgi and Shusin failed to keep them out. In some places they managed to infiltrate to such an extent that during the reign of Ibbisin, the last of the rulers in Ur, a member of these groups by the name of Ishbi-Erra took control of the city of Isin. From there, he gradually persuaded major parts of the realm to break with the central government. Decisive support was granted by Enlil, the highest god, as revealed in an exchange of letters between Ishbi-Erra of Isin, the city ruler of Kazallu, and Ibbisin. While admitting that Enlil was favoring Ishbi-Erra, Ibbisin asserts that Enlil will turn his face to him once again.In the meantime, Ishbi-Erra was making headway, and he was able to win the support also of other cities as well as Kazallu. Ibbisins's precarious situation is shown by his request of Ishbi-Erra to deliver a large amount of barley, which he says he has already paid for. As we know from other sources, Ur was facing a severe famine.

Before this conflict could be resolved, the Elamites, from the area bordering Babylonia to the east, raided Babylonia, whose internal struggles had rendered it powerless, destroyed Ur, and abducted Ibbisin to Elam.

Just in time, Enlil had apparently turned his face to those forces that were likely to be victorious; but relations between the priests represented by Enlil, on the one hand, and the central rulers, on the other, had already been strained. Thus siding with the enemy of the central ruler would solve that problem. From Shulgi on, all the kings of the Third Dynasty of Ur had deified themselves, gaining the title "God of his Country." The governor of Eshnunna dedicated a temple attached to his palace to "Shusin, his god," as we know from a foundation inscription. While we do not know how the priests reacted to this countrywide worship of the deified kings, we have already suggested that *The Curse of Akkad* was meant to warn the Ur III rulers not to overstep the mark.

During the final years of Ibbisin's reign, Ishbi-Erra had laid claim to the succession, as evidenced by his adoption of the entire set of titles, including self-deification. After the expulsion of the Elamites from Ur, he gained full control. The actual extent of his power is unclear, however, since local rule was established around that time in Larsa, which within few generations became a dangerously competing power. Over several decades, the conflict between the cities of Isin and Larsa kept smoldering, though not escalating, because Isin was located on the western branch of the Euphrates and Larsa was on the eastern branch, so that their irrigation areas were separated.

When fighting started between the two cities, Babylon intervened, being in a stronger position than either of the others as it sat upstream on the Euphrates. After the elimination of Isin by Sinmuballit, Hammurapi's father, Larsa proved a serious rival, not least by drawing its power from a temporary coalition with Elam. When Hammurapi became king of Babylon, he resorted to a measure that may have been used before. From our knowledge of a heavy famine in Larsa and, especially, from Hammurapi's note of the thirty-third year of reign that "he made abundant water reach Nippur, Eridu, Ur, Larsa, Uruk, and Isin and caused the shattered Sumer and Akkad to return to their former condition," we may deduce that the flow of water into the south had earlier been interrupted, presumably by being diverted or because the dikes of the Euphrates in Hammurapi's territory had not been repaired.

After a period during which political power was divided among several city-states, Hammurapi became the third ruler to unite Babylonia. According to the introduction to his codex, Marduk, the city god of Babylon, had conferred "enlilness over mankind" upon him (fig. 48). But conditions had changed since the time of the early central states. Both Akkad and Ur III fall into the period of Babylonia's unchallenged supremacy over its neighbors. Depending on their power, rulers had made incursions of varying dura-

FIGURE 48. Upper part of the stela containing Hammurapi's codex, ca. 1800 BCE (total height: 225 cm)

tion into these neighboring regions. By the Third Dynasty of Ur, however, city-states in the area of modern Syria had reorganized themselves, each with extensive hinterland, and were making use of the simplified script of the Ur III administration. Assur and Elam too had regained power. All at once, Hammurapi found himself surrounded by political entities that were dangerous enough to require protective measures. To this end, Hammurapi sought to extend his territory by conquering Assur, Mari, and Eshnunna. Unintentionally, his action marked the beginning of the end, for it destroyed the buffer zones that kept would-be invaders away from

FIGURE 49. Modern impression of a seal from the time of Hammurapi, ca. 1800 BCE

his borders. By the time of his successors, the new areas were already lost; a local power even managed to set up an obscure regime in southern Babylonia, the Dynasty of the Sea Land.

Around 1700 BCE at the latest, the Hittites and the political entities of Assur, Susa, Yamkhad, and Qatna began altering the power structure of the Near East. Babylonia had lost its peculiar political role under Hammurapi's successors. When in 1595 BCE, under mysterious circumstances, the Hittite ruler Murshili made an incursion as far as Babylon, he inflicted a serious blow to the formerly dominant power, from which it did not recover for many years.

The new Amoritic groups strongly characterized what is known as the Old Babylonian period. In time, almost all local and territorial rulers were members of these groups, to judge by their names. The changes that occurred, however, resulted less from their presence than from continuous developments or responses to particular situations. For instance, the change in the way that employees of temple and palace were paid—from rations to a system of self-reliance with the help of official land allotted to them—was probably an answer to the rigid system of distribution of the Ur III period.

Our sources are exceptionally good for the early part of the second millennium. Because many settlements either were abandoned after this period or survived only on a smaller scale, their remains are easily accessible. Yet it is not just by chance that many letters have been found in both official and private archives that for the first time offer insights into everyday life. The most famous of these archives is the gigantic collection of letters stored in the royal palace at Mari, which contains, along with official and private correspondence, a large corpus of women's correspondence.

The first mathematical texts date from this period, anticipating the law of Pythagoras. Yet calculations of all kinds, such as estimating labor quotas or determining the size of fields dating back to earlier periods, show that people of this era had long been acquainted with various arithmetic operations and were quite capable of solving mathematical problems at hand.

Also part of a long tradition was Hammurapi's famous code of law (fig. 48). Though it is the only such code preserved almost completely, direct precursors go back to the time of Urnamma, of the Third Dynasty of Ur.

A number of gods, known earlier only in the areas to the west, now made their appearance in Babylonia, no doubt introduced by the Amorites when they infiltrated the country. Among them were many weather deities, a group that for some reason had played no significant role in Babylonia before.

Few examples of large-scale art have survived from this period. The scene decorating the upper part of Hammurapi's law stela, depicting the investiture of the king by the sun god Shamash (fig. 48), shows a return to natural bodily proportions. Many and varied, on the other hand, are examples of the miniature art of cylinder seals (fig. 49). The presentation scene remained predominant, but a number of new themes appeared that were related to the worldview of the new groups. By comparison with those of the Ur III period, fewer seals now bore inscriptions, but the variety of seal designs increased. New ways of combining parts of different themes were devised. Unlike the earlier custom of depicting only closed themes, to which all elements would belong, we now frequently find "filling motifs"—isolated objects, small human or animal figures, or parts of a more complete theme—combined in the image on a seal. These unrelated parts were likely citations from a whole field of themes known both to the artists and to their customers, thus offering an unlimited range of seal designs that could easily be individualized. As in earlier situations, this development reflected the increasing number of people engaged in economic affairs who needed clearly identifiable seals.

6 Babylonia as Part of the Near Eastern Community of States (1595–1200 BCE)

The Hittite ruler Murshili's raid on Babylon at the beginning of the sixteenth century BCE marks more than the end of the First Dynasty of Babylon. It signals a change of paradigm in the history of the ancient Near East. For more than fifteen hundred years, Babylonia had been the prime mover at all levels—admittedly in frequent and direct exchange with its neighbors. Toward the end of the First Dynasty of Babylon, other powers attracted attention, whether for a relatively short time, like Elam and Assur, or as harbingers or representatives of longer-term developments, like the Syrian states or the Hittites. After the middle of the second millennium, the power structure of the entire Near East was finally reorganized. In this process, Babylonia was assigned a new and remarkable role: within a large area it remained the cultural point of reference—in script, literature, religion, or art—but with respect to power politics it lost its dominance; at best, it was merely on a par with several other political entities.

From the sixteenth and fifteenth centuries BCE, so little information has survived that we hesitate to reconstruct even the sequence of rulers. This period has been called a dark age, but the paucity of records should not make us think that the administrative and cultural achievements of earlier times had fallen apart. On the contrary, the numerous sources from about 1400 BCE on reveal so much continuity that we need an explanation for the previous lack of useful documents.

Since a number of settlements were abandoned after the period of the First Dynasty of Babylon, remains from that time lie close to the surface and are easily accessible. The settlements that survived into the following Kassite period, on the other hand, were occupied over long periods and thus accumulated layers of occupational debris. Consequently, remains from the Kassite period are normally many meters below the surface. In Babylon especially, which should furnish the most interesting documents, these levels are almost inaccessibly deep and in groundwater. An exception is the city of Dur-Kurigalzu (now Aqar Quf, west of Baghdad), founded by the Kassite king Kurigalzu I as his royal seat. Because economic life may have been less centralized at the time, and economic units smaller, people may not have bothered to use writing unless they had no choice. A most interesting find should be mentioned here: a clay container from this period contained a number of numerical tokens resembling those we encountered from the fourth millennium. So those simple devices for storing information were still in use centuries after the availability of writing.

The cultural-political continuity is particularly striking in light of language changes. With the Kassites, a new population element again assumed dominance; but unlike the earlier Amorites, who at least spoke a Semitic language closely related to the main languages of Babylonia, the Kassites spoke an entirely foreign language. Unfortunately, all we can say is that it bore no relation to any of the known families of languages, for hardly anything has survived other than personal names and a few other words. According to their tradition, the Kassites came from the eastern mountains. Kassite names had already turned up in Babylonia during the reign of Hammurapi; they grew more numerous in connection with a small political unit by the name of Khana, whose capital, Terqa, lay on the middle Euphrates. The fall of Babylon that resulted from Murshili's invasion opened the way for the Kassites to seize power in Babylon. While we have no details, it seems reasonable to assume some kind of cooperation with Murshili, since the Hittites had to pass through Khana.

The names of early Kassite kings are known only from a king list of later date. But this does not imply their insignificance, as illustrated by King Karaindash from the end of the fifteenth century BCE. Karaindash even took over the entire set of titles used since the Third Dynasty of Ur. Apparently Uruk was part of his realm, which was administered from Babylon. According to inscriptions

FIGURE 50. Reconstructed facade of the temple of Karaindash in Uruk, made of molded bricks (presumed height of the figures: 205 cm).

found in Uruk, Karaindash remodeled the ziqqurrat and built a small temple dedicated to Inanna, the city goddess of Uruk. This temple, which has been fully excavated, presents a plan so different from normal Babylonian temples that it may represent one of the few items we can genuinely call Kassite. The way the outer facades are decorated with reliefs was also novel (fig. 50). The construction technique, however, using pre-molded bricks, had a long local tradition.

Although the first half of the fourteenth century is hardly known from documents of its own, light is shed in an unusual manner by external sources. In the palace of Tell el-Amarnah in Egypt, the royal seat founded by the pharaoh Akhenaten (1353–1336 BCE), 350 clay tablets have been found, written in cuneiform and representing a correspondence between pharaohs and Near Eastern rulers. Most of the correspondents were rulers of small city-states and political units in the region of Syro-Palestine, but a few were Babylonian kings. Pharaohs and Babylonian kings call each other "brother," apparently recognizing each other as equal; they exchange gifts and make requests of each other. For instance, the pharaohs ask for Kassite princesses, while the Kassite kings are more interested in deliveries of gold. These mutual interests indicate that Kassite Babylonia occupied an established place within the network of Near Eastern and Egyptian powers.

The Kassites represented one more group from the eastern mountains that made a massive imprint on Mesopotamian affairs; another group, the Hurrians, will be discussed below. Some of these groups made short-term raids into the Mesopotamian lowlands, but others apparently planned to settle there permanently. The Elamites are the group we know best because of written sources ranging over different periods; they had a culture of their own, which often interconnected closely with Babylonian culture. Groups like the Guti can be traced only as long as they remained in Babylonia; no other records of their doings survive. Of the Lullubi we have at least one piece of evidence from their area of origin, for Anubanini, one of their "kings," immortalized himself in a rock relief near modern Sar-i Pol-e Zohab, close to Qasr Shirin. We know nothing about the area the Kassites came from; it was probably north of the Lullubi territory and thus difficult to distinguish from that of the Hurrians.

These groups are often spoken of as "marginal," as failing to reach a higher level of civilization in their native area, because little or nothing is known about them before they entered the Mesopotamian lowlands. But this constant movement toward the plains should not be attributed merely to an inclination to raid neighboring lands but should also be seen as part of the age-old process of interchange between mountains and lowlands. In earlier periods this exchange had contributed immensely to the development of the entire area. Even the massive settlement of the Babylonian plain of the middle of the fourth millennium may have been part of this process. Tempted by the written record, we have understandably—but in a biased manner—internalized the viewpoint of the lowland inhabitants.

For the first time during the Akkadian period we meet people with Hurrian names in Babylonia, where they had been brought as prisoners of war. Yet only in the sixteenth century BCE did they come to the fore as founders of the emerging Mittani kingdom and form part of the population in the regions between the coast of the Mediterranean and the Zagros Mountains. We know them from written sources found in Qatna and Alalakh in western Syria but also from the many documents found in Nuzi in the vicinity of modern Kirkuk. Adopting the Mesopotamian cuneiform writing, the Hurrians also took over Mesopotamian language and literature, but at the same time they made use of the script for their own language, producing a literature of their own. This development must have been preceded by a long process of infiltration and expansion, which we call silent because it has not found reflection in any existing written sources or archaeological traces.

It is particularly enigmatic that in the emergence of the Mittani state at the end of the sixteenth century BCE, the normal Hurrian population came to be dominated by a ruling class whose personal names proved to be of Indo-Aryan origin; the same was true of the gods they worshiped. Examples are Artatama, Tushratta, and Shattiwaza, or the divine names Mitra, Varuna, and Indra. The contacts between Hurrians and Indo-Aryan groups may go back to a time when both groups lived in the region of what is now Iran, before the migration of Indo-Aryan groups eastward toward the Indus valley, and of the Hurrian groups westward.

The history of the Hurrian states is closely linked to those of the Hittites. Again, the origin and early history of the Hittites remain obscure, but at least from the middle of the seventeenth century BCE an empire had been established in central Anatolia, with its capital Hattusha. Since the Hittite empire, throughout its lifetime, exhibited an urge to expand southward toward of the plains of northern Syria, conflicts with the local Hurrian states and the subsequent Mittani state were predictable.

By the end of the sixteenth and the beginning of the fifteenth century BCE, another power tried to gain a foothold in Syria: Thutmosis III (1479–1427 BCE) of Egypt succeeded in conquering parts of Syrian territory and restraining the influence of Mittani. There were hints of a possible alliance between Egypt and the bordering states of the Hittites, Assur (fig. 51), and Babylonia, so as to curb Mittani; but the Mittani ruler Saushtatar was soon able to regain his state's former possessions on the Mediterranean coast. He even managed to conquer Assur and to seize power over the kingdom of Arrapkha, the area around modern Kirkuk.

So far, Assur has turned up primarily as the name of a city,

FIGURE 51. Main part of the city of Assur

which was conquered at various times by the rulers of the Third Dynasty of Ur, or by Hammurapi of Babylon, but never became part of their core territory. According to archaeological findings, inhabitants of the area during the first half of the third millennium had settled on a rocky promontory projecting into the Tigris river plain. By the middle of that millennium the city seems already to have gained some importance.

Between 1920 and 1860 BCE, Assur must have been an important trade hub, which could not have succeeded without a certain political backing. Unfortunately the evidence comes not from Assur itself but from trade colonies in what is now eastern Anatolia, where Assyrian merchants did business. In their living quarters outside the walls of the local towns—as for instance in Kanesh (now Kultepe, northeast of Kayseri)—they left thousands of trade documents. Trade goods were mainly textiles and tin, probably from Babylonia and the eastern mountains, which the merchants exchanged for gold and silver. A number of such trade stations in Anatolia, like one in Hattusha, which subsequently became the capital of the Hittite empire, show the breadth of the trade network controlled by the Assyrian merchants (fig. 52).

After centuries during which the lack of written information probably reflected the city's minor importance, Assur regained

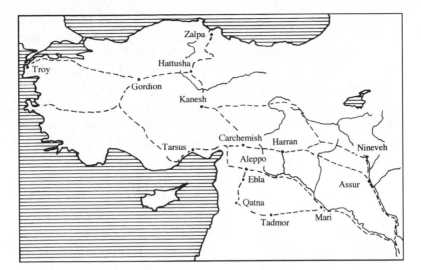

FIGURE 52. Trade routes of Assyrian merchants in the nineteenth century BCE

some standing in the fourteenth century BCE, when it became a power center under the rulers Eriba-Adad (1390–1365) and, especially, his son Assur-uballit I (1365–1328). In his correspondence with the pharaoh Akhenaten, Assur-uballit I calls himself "King of Kings" and acts on the same level as Burnaburiash, king of Babylon, to whom he gave a daughter in marriage. Still, his territory seems to have had narrow limits, for when the ailing pharaoh Amenophis III requested that he send him the healing cult-statue of Ishtar of Niniveh, the sender was not Assur-uballit but the king of Mittani.

The marriage alliance between Babylon and Assur did not last long, since one son of this marriage was murdered shortly after he had succeeded his father as king, and a second son, called Kurigalzu, who was appointed king of Babylon by Assur-uballit, subsequently turned against his grandfather. It was the first in a long series of attempts by Assyrian kings to exert influence on Babylon.

For the time being, the various powers kept each other in check and made sure that none of the units grew too powerful. An alliance with the Hittites, for instance, gave Kurigalzu enough backing to be able to march against Assur and subsequently to defeat Elam, always ready to form an alliance with Assur.

Elam turned out to be another actor in the grand power play at the end of which Assur emerged as victor at the beginning of the first millennium. Controlling the fertile plain of today's southwestern Iran, along with the extensive hinterland, rich in raw materials, that sometimes extended as far as Seistan, Elam always had the potential of playing a major role. But it played that role inconsistently: its interests were split between Khuzestan, which normally was fully integrated into Mesopotamian life and culture, and a hinterland belonging to an area that, with the other parts of Iran, Afghanistan, Beluchistan, and the Indus valley, formed a cultural space of its own and had occasional connections to developments in central Asia.

Elam would enter the picture if tempted by political or economic weakness in Assyria or Babylonia to raid their territories. It may even have considered remaining there for an extended period. More than once, if one part of Mesopotamia had to defend itself against the other, Elam was a welcome partner.

At certain times, the entire Near East including Egypt had been part of a cultural entity. In the Amarnah correspondence, not only cuneiform writing but even the Babylonian language was used as a lingua franca between, for example, a pharaoh and a Palestinian ruler, neither of whom spoke Babylonian as a mother tongue. And it was certainly more than coincidence that rulers of such distant regions as Babylonia, Egypt, Elam, and Assyria should found new cities as their royal seats within the span of a century and a half. The ruling figures seemed to share a widespread change in self-conception.

The Kassite king Kurigalzu I (around 1390) opened a series of city building by founding Dur-Kurigalzu (now Aqar Quf, west of Baghdad) as a sprawling palace and temple city. He was followed by the pharaoh Amenophis IV (1353–1336), who under the name of Akhenaten built Akhetaten (now Tell el-Amarnah). The Elamite ruler Untash-Napirisha (1260–1235) erected the palace and temple city of Dur-Untash (modern Chogha Zanbil in Khuzestan). And last in line, though almost a contemporary of Untash-Napirisha, was the Assyrian king Tukulti-Ninurta I (1243–1207), who built his new city Kar-Tukulti-Ninurta on the banks of the Tigris, opposite Assur. Akhenaten and Tukulti-Ninurta are known to have sought an escape from the bustle of their old capitals, hoping to make a fresh start. For Akhenaten, furthermore, the project was part of his program of reforms, which were intended to reorganize state and cult.

All four of these new foundations scarcely survived their patrons: Dur-Kurigalzu never succeeded in finding its place besides Babylon—only the temples retained some importance—and Akhetaten was totally abandoned after the failure of the reforms. Dur Untash never rivaled Susa, and only the impressive building of the Ziqqurrat kept its memory alive. Kar-Tukulti-Ninurta remained settled for a while, though on a fraction of the area originally planned, as indicated by the city wall; but again, except in its initial phase, it was never a challenge for Assur. As we will see shortly, the habit of founding new seats of power was continued only in Assyria, where the kings of the Neo-Assyrian empire competed in out-doing their predecessors with the erection of new palaces.

A growing self-assurance is also reflected in the art pertaining to the reigns of Eriba-Adad and Assur-uballit. It is particularly noticeable on cylinder seals, the only examples of art preserved in considerable numbers. Seal art of the Mittani period had adopted elements of all the styles that existed previously in the realm, including styles affiliated with the Syrian, Assyrian, and even Babylonian regions (fig. 53a). The seals follow a custom we have met before, that of presenting a major theme such as like the veneration of a leader or a god and placing it side by side with elements of other themes. This is why seals from the Mittani period rarely hang together coherently. The single elements seem to be strewn haphazardly over the entire seal surface, an impression intensified by the absence of dividing lines as means of organization.

A radical change occurs with king Eriba-Adad, whose royal seal shows a clear, heraldic arrangement with all elements belonging to the same theme: two winged demons supporting a winged sun disk (fig. 53b). This new style not only remained in use by Eriba-Adad's successors but was soon taken up by the inhabitants of the city of Assur. People in the surrounding villages, however, who occasionally had to use their seals for signing documents drawn up by merchants from Assur, retained their old-style seals for a while.

FIGURE 53. Seal of the Mittani king Saushtatar, fifteenth century BCE; and seal of the Assyrian king Eriba-Adad, fourteenth century BCE

The new mentality is reflected not only in the application of symmetric principles of arrangement but even more in the treatment of the figures, which are clearly outlined and stand out against the background. For the first time since the Akkadian period, the background became an active element, and flat spaces were integrated into the composition. Indeed, the rapid change in art at the beginning of the Akkadian period may have been as consciously steered by the rulers as it was now by Eriba-Adad.

The common mentality of Assyria and Babylonia was nowhere more clearly manifested than in religion. Along with the city god Assur, all the great Babylonian gods were present in Assyria, even in their traditional rank order. Enlil, the highest god of the Babylonian pantheon, was held in particular reverence. It was to him that the ziqqurrat, the largest temple in Assur, was dedicated, and Assyrian kings from Eriba-Adad onward assumed "regent of Enlil" as their primary title.

Under king Shalmaneser I, Enlil was equated with Assur, who by that time had been promoted to imperial god. Now it was Assur who led the Assyrian army into battle, thereby lending a religious dimension to military campaigns. Unlike Enlil, he had become the god in whose name wars were fought. In the same spirit, conquered areas were now incorporated into the victor's own territory, whereas former military campaigns had been little more than raids, or had been waged against rebel vassals.

During his wars of conquest, Shalmaneser for the first time encountered an enemy who was to play a major role in the years to come: the Aramaeans, then living in today's Syria. After the destruction of what remained of the state of Mittani, petty states had formed around important cities such as Aleppo, Karkemish, and Til Barsip under the leadership of members of those tribes known under the collective name of Aramaeans. Fighting the Ahlamu, as they called themselves, became part of the normal military agenda of Assyrian kings. The constant oscillation between attacking the Aramaeans—who stood in the way of westward expansion—and defending against attacks from their side made for a precarious situation.

In Babylonia, however, things seem to have been generally calm, except for occasional raids by the Elamites from the east. The triangle between Babylonia, Elam, and Assyria grew turbulent again when Tukulti-Ninurta I, the son of Shalmaneser, raided Babylonia, which had been weakened by an Elamite raid, and abducted the Kassite ruler to Assyria. Sixty years later, after Babylon had been raided by an Assyrian king, Elam took advantage of the internal power struggle to establish a permanent rule in Babylon. In light of the perpetual skirmishing, this raid would not be worth mentioning if it had not been accompanied by another "first": the Elamite king Shutruk-Nahhunte was the first known monarch to use a military campaign for large-scale pillaging of art objects.

Statues and reliefs encountered in the conquered Babylonian cities were brought into Shutruk-Nahhunte's capital, Susa, where some of them received his own inscriptions, and were placed in the king's palace. More than three thousand years later, at the end of the nineteenth century CE, they were taken from that site by a French archaeological expedition and transferred to the Louvre. Among them are some of the most famous pieces of art from ancient Mesopotamia, including Naramsin's victory stela and the stela containing the Codex Hammurapi (figs. 44 and 48). It is striking to see the importance attached to art for creating an identity, and the extent to which its loss meant—and was supposed to mean—a loss of identity. It is also striking, from a historical point of view, that artworks already a thousand years old in Shutruk-Nahhunte's time were still visibly exposed, making them easy prey.

For the second half of the 2nd millennium BCE, we have a general picture of Babylonia as politically weak, owing to frequent raids on its territory or even attempts by outsiders to gain

FIGURE 54. A *kudurru,* with text
of a land contract, ca. 1100 BCE

a permanent foothold there. We should not overlook, however, Babylonia's cultural creativity during this period. For example, a new type of monument called a *kudurru* emerged (fig. 54). On these standing stones, the texts of land contracts were written, which led to their false categorization as boundary stones. Another part of the stone would be occupied by images, normally consisting of emblems of the gods. These emblems served the same purpose as the gods whose names followed the inscription: to guarantee the contract.

The literary tradition was considered so important during the Kassite period that it was virtually canonized in order to be preserved. From the many versions and independent parts of major literary works, permanent texts were established, mostly taking on the form in which they have survived. To this end, the scribes had to study the old literature, possibly including texts written in a script that was no longer fully understood. These efforts may have necessitated the creation of dictionaries like the one mentioned in chapter 3, which translated the first entry of the ancient list of titles by the later term "king."

The resurgence of Assyrian power, the appearance of the Aramaeans, and the constant but unsuccessful attempts of Assyria to control Babylonia are three major themes that will be examined in depth in chapter 7. The balance between a number of middle-range powers, none of which was able to act by itself, was knocked out of kilter by the dissolution of the Mittani state shortly after 1300 BCE and, more particularly, by the swift and surprising end of the Hittite empire around 1200. Taking advantage of this vacuum. and supported by an imperial god and an imperial ideology, Assyria governed the subsequent development of Mesopotamia and the Near East in general.

7 The Empires of the Assyrians and the Babylonians (1200–539 BCE)

Any attempt to write history based on written or archaeological evidence has to grapple with the question of what the ancients thought fit to write down, and what might have left traces recoverable by archaeological methods. Severe limits are also posed by the lack of texts in which writers reflect on their own history. Instead, we find intellectual or religious concepts disguised in epics or myths; or texts presenting themselves as historical accounts, which quite often turn out to be outright propaganda. Almost by definition, royal inscriptions mention only those events that enhance the ruler's prestige. And there is a tendency, in both ancient and modern times, to judge a ruler's importance only by wars and military successes. By following too closely the presentation of the authors of official inscriptions, we risk underestimating the importance of certain periods because they lack full written coverage or because no wars or conquests are mentioned. Yet extended periods of peace, even if unrecorded, are certainly noteworthy. The time around 1000 BCE seems to have constituted such a period in Mesopotamia: uneventful but peaceful.

The Kassite dynasty in Babylon had come to an end in 1157 as a result of a raid by the Elamites. Of subsequent rulers, combined into a dynasty of Isin by a later king list, very little is known other than name and duration of reign as recorded in the king list. Yet at one time they must have been strong enough to recapture the statue of Marduk, which had been taken to Susa.

A quiet period for Assyria is indicated by the fact that Assur-rabi II (1010–970) reigned for forty years without major events worth mentioning. Only when his successors were on the throne

FIGURE 55. Stone relief from the palace at Calah of the Assyrian king Assurnasirpal II, showing the king with two servants

do we hear of new fights with the Aramaeans to the west and with the mountain tribes to the east. At the beginning of the ninth century BCE, "kings" are mentioned for the first time with respect to the area of the eastern mountains, which suggests that political structures were being formed among the tribes as a measure to defend off the Assyrian pressure.

We are better informed about the reign of Assurnasirpal II (883–859). Besides his far-reaching military campaigns, inscriptions refer to the transformation of a formerly unimportant settlement into his new capital, Calah (now Nimrud). Situated on the eastern banks of the Tigris between Assur and the city of Nineveh, Calah received an extensive palace complex, which from now on served as the prototype of such complexes both in layout and furnishing. For the first time, walls were covered with large slabs of stone decorated with reliefs, following examples in Syria and southeastern Anatolia, giving the palace a special appearance. Various hunting and war scenes, as well as scenes of a cultic nature, center around the representation of the king, in full royal regalia, with rich embroidered robes and finely engraved ornaments (fig. 55). The basic material of the reliefs was the fine-grained Mosul alabaster, which lends itself to minutely detailed work. The reliefs were painted in bright colors, preserved only in faint traces. Visitors were supposed to be intimidated by the reliefs with their sometimes larger-than-life figures, not to mention the human-headed bull figures that flanked the entrances and passages of the palace (fig. 56).

FIGURE 56. Guardian figure in the form of a bull-man, one of a pair flanking the gates of the palace of Sargon II at Dur-Sharrukin (height: 420 cm)

Both the maturity of the techniques and the sureness of the representation point to a long tradition of decorating walls, though preserved in Assyria only in the form of wall paintings and a wall covered with colored glazed bricks in Tukulti-Ninurta's late thirteenth-century palace.

Assurnasirpal's palace exemplifies for first time the combination of immense vigor and incredible ruthlessness characteristic of all subsequent rulers of Assyria, for it was completed, with all its decoration and furnishings, only four years after Assurnasirpals's ascent to the throne in 879. The same speed and drive were also apparent in the execution of his military campaigns. Contending with unending conflicts and sieges, his army had to cover impressive distances. Five years after his accession, Assurnasirpal not only had subdued the resistance of the Aramaic states but had advanced with his army to the coast of the Mediterranean. His appearance must have been intimidating enough to cause the Phoenician cities to offer tribute to him without any military action. The mobility of the Assyrian army resulted partly from military reforms, which put greater emphasis on the chariot contingents, and partly from constantly advancing the supply depots in order to keep supply routes short.

Equally impressive were the distances covered by Assurnasirpals's son and successor Shalmaneser III (858–824), who advanced four times to Cilicia, in addition to waging major or minor campaigns against the Aramaic states and the emerging political structures in the eastern mountains. For the first time, a territory called Parsuash is mentioned, which is assumed to be the earliest reference to the land of the Persians. Apparently an important aim of the campaigns was the amassing of all kinds of booty, as illustrated on the palace reliefs. Entire herds of cattle and many other items were dragged off from conquered cities. An enormous arsenal built by Shalmaneser in Calah contained, in addition to new weapons and others taken from defeated forces, thousands of ivory plaques, which once adorned pieces of furniture, or were intended for that purpose. To judge from their style, showing many Syrian and Egyptian elements, they probably represent booty from the Syrian campaigns.

Since the time of Shalmaneser I in the thirteenth century BCE, Assyrian military actions commonly included the forced relocation of fairly large groups of inhabitants from conquered areas to Assyria. These actions were supposed not only to weaken local opposition against Assyrian control but also to reinforce the workforce in Assyria. It appears that craftsmen in particular were imported for the huge building projects. These groups populated the new capital cities like Kar-Tukulti-Ninurta or Calah.

This policy of moving and resettling people had unforeseen consequences from the ninth century BCE on. Many of these groups originated from the Aramaic speaking areas; they spoke a West Semitic language close related to, but also significantly different from East Semitic Assyrian. Under the influence of Aramaic on everyday language, a slow but continuous process of an Aramaization transformed the Assyrian language: not only did numerous Aramaic loan words appear in Assyrian, but there were even syntactic changes.

The relationship between Babylonia and Assyria changed as a consequence of Shamshi-Adad V's laying claim to Babylonia following a raid in 818 BCE. Subsequent Assyrian rulers followed his lead. Since the middle of the second millennium, the peculiar relation between the two parts of Mesopotamia had always been governed by the military supremacy of Assyria and the cultural supremacy of Babylonia. Although Assyria's efforts to expand its territory in all directions naturally affected Babylonia, respect for the country of origin of one's own culture prevented Babylonia from being treated the same way as the other areas under Assyrian military control. For the same reason, however, Babylonia's continuous attempts to get rid of the Assyrian supremacy were seen as family betrayal and punished more severely than resistance from other areas.

Since around 1000 BCE, Babylonia had undergone substantial changes. A long development had started toward the end of the eighteenth century and the beginning of the seventeenth, when the city of Babylon became the political capital of the country, cementing the shift of power to the northern part of Babylonia. A kind of inner colonization of northern Babylonia was effected by means of new canals and the founding of new settlements—all at the expense of the south, which now received less water. As mentioned earlier, a "Dynasty of the Sea Land" had been established somewhere in the south during the later part of the First Dynasty of Babylon, though apparently without a main settlement or capital. Some southern areas may have been under the control of tribes. In the territory around Uruk, rural settlements in the second half of the second millennium were exceedingly sparse. The population of this period seems to have concentrated in cities like Ur, Uruk, Isin, Larsa, and Nippur.

This relatively thin rural population was taken advantage of during this period by Aramaean and Chaldaean tribes, who migrated from the northwest and established political entities of their own in the south. With names such as Bit Adini or Bit Amukani (*bit,* from *bitu,* meaning "house," plus the tribal name), they may be identified as tribal areas. Nothing is known about urban centers or fixed boundaries.

Thus, during the beginning of the first millennium BCE, Babylonia consisted of three parts: the tribal areas of the Aramaeans and Chaldaeans, the cities of southern Babylonia, and—in population and economic power the most important of the three—northern Babylonia. In their attempts to control Babylonia, the Assyrians had to deal with the tribes, who by definition always wanted to demonstrate their independence; with the southern cities, which, as potential springboards for tribal resistance, had to go along with the tribes; and with the north, which would be readier than the other areas to recognize Assyrian supremacy for economic reasons. The Assyrians managed to secure their rule by setting up military garrisons in the southern cities, recognizing that they would never be able to control the tribes directly. In this constellation it was natural, if ironic, that almost all serious attempts to oppose the Assyrian presence and regain Babylonia's independence were launched by members of the tribes.

It was during this period that the short reign of Shammuramat occurred; the only queen to occupy the Assyrian throne, she ruled between 810 and 806, until her minor son, Adadnirari III, was ready to take over. Under the name of Semiramis she is said to have become the wife of the Chaldaean ruler Nebuchadnezzar II, but since he lived 200 years later, the story is clearly apocryphal.

Assyria attained the greatest expansion it had known so far during the rule of Tiglath-Pileser III (744–727), who claimed all of modern Syria as far as Samaria, the Phoenician cities, and southeastern Anatolia up to the river Halys (now called Kızıl Irmak) to be part of his realm. He declared the "blue mountain" (now Demavend, northeast of Teheran) as the eastern border of his area of influence. In 733 BCE he made innovative use of the turmoils surrounding the throne in Babylon to assume power over the whole of Babylonia: under the name of Pulu he enthroned himself king of Babylon, inaugurating a series of dual monarchs while acknowledging the special role of Babylonia, which could thus maintain the illusion of being independent and having a king of its own.

The next but one of the Assyrian rulers was Sargon II (721–705). He revealed himself to be a usurper by taking the name *sharru kenu*, "legitimate king," a deliberate reference to the founder of the Akkadian empire almost sixteen hundred years earlier, who was still remembered. Sargon II expanded his Palestinian possessions by a province centered on the city of Ashdod, and made a first but unsuccessful attempt to conquer Egypt. Toward the north and the east, local centers of power had emerged, notably one in the area around Lake Van in eastern Anatolia. This state, called Urartu, had already grown to be a competitor; around 840 BCE, its first

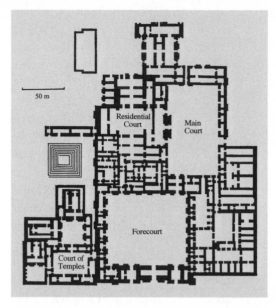

FIGURE 57. Palace of Sargon II at Dur-Sharrukin

king, Sarduri, used the title of "King of the Universe," leaving no doubt as to his ambitions. Sargon, however, was able to defeat Urartu and at the same time to push back the Cimmerians, who, under pressure from the Scythians, breathing down their neck, had invaded the area of modern Azerbaijan from the northeast.

In 721 BCE, the same year that Sargon II became king of Assyria, power over Babylonia was seized by the chief of the Chaldaean tribe of Yakin, Marduk-apal-iddina II (Merodach-baladan of the Old Testament). In 710, breaking a treaty, Sargon invaded Babylonia, expelled Marduk-apal-iddina, and destroyed the central place (we do not know its name) of Bit Yakin. The defeated monarch was forced to seek refuge in the marshes of lower Babylonia.

Sargon too built himself a new capital: Dur-Sharrukin, now called Khorsabad, not far northeast of Mosul. A wall surrounded the city of a little more than one and one-half kilometers square. An extended terrace on the northwestern side offered enough space for a temple compound for the god Nabu, for four palatial residences (one for the king's brother who was also his general), and for a second elevated terrace for the royal palace proper (fig. 57). In size as in embellishment, with its ornamented stone slabs, this

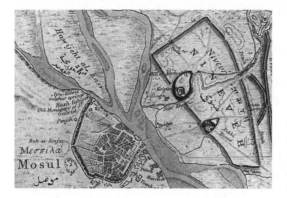

FIGURE 58. Location of the city of Nineveh (detail from Felix Jones's 1852 map of Assyria)

palace put earlier palaces in the shade. It comprised an area in which three deities could be worshiped, two enormous courtyards, and the core area of the throne and banquet halls, leading into the private quarters of the royal family. Besides representations glorifying the ruler, we find detailed reports of the military campaigns, partly identified by the addition of written place- and personal names. Exhaustive reports on the building describe the construction process and, in particular, the amounts of precious materials used. The palace was inaugurated in 706 with festivities lasting several days. It was used as the seat of power for only a short time, however, for Sargon died just one year later, in 705, during another military campaign in the west, and his son Sennacherib immediately moved the seat of government to Nineveh (fig. 58), where he built himself a new palace.

Nineveh had long been the biggest city in Assyria. It had developed around two ancient settlements on two small hills, which because of a long history of habitation had attained some height. They are now known by the names of Kuyuncik and Nebi Yunus. The latter name refers to the legend of the mosque in the highest part of the settlement marking the prophet Jonah's tomb. Sennacherib (704–681 BCE) extended the unified settlement to encompass seven square kilometers, including spacious parks and gardens, all surrounded by a city wall (fig. 58). To ensure a supply of water, Sennacherib had a canal thirty kilometers long constructed, which diverted water from the Little Zab, one of the tributaries of the Tigris, into the small river flowing through the urban area of

Nineveh. At one point the canal bridged a valley by means of an aqueduct of 220 meters long and nine meters high—an unprecedented feat of engineering and another "first."

As indicated by the name "Palace without Rival," Sennacherib aspired to build a palace even larger and more splendid than his father's. As before, the reliefs portray the ruler appearing in his regalia at cultic or state performances; equally fascinating are the numerous narrative depictions, with their delicacy and love for detail. The viewer learns where various military campaigns took place by means of characteristic landscapes and local peculiarities revealed in the artwork or stated in accompanying inscriptions.

Like modern war correspondents scribbling notes and taking photographs on site to be used for later reports, those ancient reliefs show scribes with tablet and stylus, side-by-side with figures who may represent draftsmen, holding sketching materials.

Of particular importance in Sennacherib's reign, besides the normal campaigns aimed at suppressing revolts at the margins of the empire, were his actions against Babylonia. He used Marduk-apal-iddina's attempt to return to Babylon in 703 BCE as an opportunity to devastate Babylonia in an unprecedented manner, and to relocate more than two hundred thousand people to Assyria. From 691 on, however, another Chaldaean, Mushezib-Marduk, managed to rally a broad coalition reaching far into the eastern mountains and to inflict a serious defeat on Sennacherib. In 688, by way of retaliation, Sennacherib ordered the city of Babylon to be destroyed totally; he wanted no one to remember where it had stood.

The destruction of Babylon was considered blasphemous. A later report connects the murder of Sennacherib in 681 to the fact that his infamous action met with resistance in his own house. It is unclear whether the son and successor Esarhaddon (680–669) was behind the murder. He clearly opposed his father's policy, for he restored privileges to the Babylonian cities. Esarhaddon revived the institution of the dual monarchy and thus became king of Babylon as well as Assyrian ruler.

Esarhaddon conducted very extensive campaigns, bringing him once to the border of Egypt and twice deep into its interior (fig. 59). In 671, the whole of lower Egypt surrendered to him. After pil-

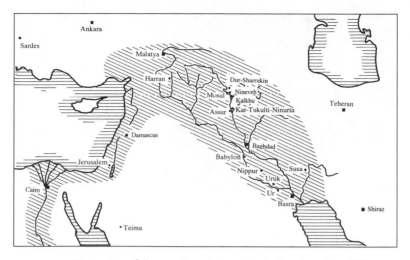

FIGURE 59. Extension of the neo-Assyrian empire during the reign of King Esarhaddon, ca. 670 BCE

laging the country, he returned to Nineveh with immense wealth. Only two years later, he renewed his campaign against Egypt, but he died before completing the mission.

The constant revolts in Babylonia had persuaded Esarhaddon that dual monarchy was not the answer. He therefore declared that he should be succeeded in Babylon by his son Shamash-shum-ukkin, and in Nineveh by his son Assurbanipal. After several years of peace, however, Shamash-shum-ukkin decided to take the lead of an anti-Assyrian faction, first instigating a revolt and then provoking a four-year war. At the war's end, Assurbanipal and his troops occupied Babylon and again devastated the city. Shamash-shum-ukkin died during the action. Assurbanipal resumed the custom of dual monarchy and, under the name of Kandalanu, made himself king of Babylon.

Like his predecessors, Assurbanipal (668–626 BCE) was involved in many far-flung actions, not least in order to retain control over Egypt, which nevertheless was lost in 655. Other campaigns were directed toward Elam and the mountainous areas to the east. Apart from these military activities, we associate his name with two accomplishments: the building and adornment of his palace, and the establishment of a library.

FIGURE 60. Section of a lion-hunting relief from Assurbanipal's palace at Nineveh

Though retaining Nineveh as capital, Assurbanipal built himself a new palace, likewise on the hill of Kuyuncik. The palace must have been even more splendid than the previous one, but unfortunately it has been poorly preserved. Long series of reliefs show the king in his official world and portray his military campaigns, but the reliefs are best known for the magnificent hunting scenes. Lions, onagers, and gazelles were apparently hunted in fenced-in areas into which the animals were released from cages. The king would shoot from a safe distance with bow and arrow. The animals are depicted as either roaming around or, after being wounded, in varying stages of dying (fig. 60). The subtlety of observation, the naturalistic depiction of the animals, and the free composition of the scenes, all rendered in stone, make these reliefs some of the most impressive creations of ancient Near Eastern art.

Our knowledge of a large part of Mesopotamian literature is owed to the discovery of the library in Assurbanipal's palace. Learned, and literate, Assurbanipal ordered old written material from all over Mesopotamia to be copied and incorporated into his library. The entire wisdom and scholarship of the age was embodied there: omen texts; texts of astronomy, astrology, and medicine; instructions for rituals and incantations; and, above all, great works of literature—the creation epic and the Gilgamesh epic, to name only two.

Not much is known about Assurbanipal's final years. When in 627 BCE one of his sons, Sin-shar-ishkun, ascended the Assyrian throne, he soon had to cope with major challenges that had been brewing for some time. In 626, the Chaldaean tribal chief Nabopolassar had proclaimed himself king of Babylon, and there was unrest among the tribes in the eastern mountains. In 616, a large coalition consisting of Elam and a number of additional groups from the Zagros, primarily the Medes and apparently including a contingent of Babylonians, attacked Assyria from the southeast. Another Babylonian contingent advanced up the Euphrates and the Habur, attacking the Assyrian mainland from the west. The city of Assur was conquered in 614, and after the Babylonian and the Median armies had joined forces, Nineveh fell in 612.

Once again, it is perplexing to observe how rapidly the Assyrian empire came to an end, only a hundred years after its immense display of power, when even Egypt was part of the empire. True, the coalition armies were more numerous and less exhausted than the Assyrian army. But, as often in similar cases, the final battles merely accelerated processes that had been developing for a number of reasons.

One of the main reasons was that the geography and thus the economic potential of Assyria were difficult to reconcile with its constant urge to expand. Like Babylonia, Assyria had almost no raw materials of its own, but it lay in the rain-fed area, where, in contrast to Babylonia with its irrigation, the growth of agriculture was constrained. So Assyria had only limited possibilities of producing items that might be exchanged on a large scale for the goods it needed. This unstable situation was exacerbated when Assyria's expansionist urge required major expenditures. This urge even became a royal duty to the imperial god Assur—a consequence of a religiously founded imperialism rooted in the conviction that Assur was entitled to rule the world—which set in motion a development from which there was no escape.

Forced to get access to foreign resources, Assyria was under constant stress. Conquered areas were first pillaged and then incorporated into the state, thus increasing costs of maintaining the empire. But these costs could be met only by the continuing conquest of new territories. The costs of the military apparatus and the lavish palaces probably consumed more means than could be amassed by booty and tributes. The expansion finally reached a natural limit in Egypt and the Mediterranean coast. With the

FIGURE 61. King
Nebuchadnezzar's
"Tower of Babel"
(H. Schmid's suggested
reconstruction)

conquest of Egypt, Assyria's economic and political collapse became predictable.

The end of the Assyrian empire coincided with the rise of a Chaldaean dynasty in Babylon, which lasted nearly one hundred years, having started in 626 with Nabopolassar. After the campaign that the Chaldaeans had jointly conducted with the Medes, the former Assyrian territory was divided into a northern part for the Medes, comprising Harran and Asia Minor, and a southern part for the Chaldaeans, consisting of Syria and Palestine and to be ruled by Nabopolassar. In the meantime, Egypt had conquered Palestine and a part of Syria; but Nebuchadnezzar, Nabopolassar's son and also his general, was able to drive the Egyptians back and even to recapture Palestine in 604. When Jerusalem failed to send the tribute due, the city was taken in 597, and a part of the population was transported to Babylonia and held captive there, as reported in the Old Testament. Ten years later, the same thing happened.

Large, rich areas acknowledged the supremacy of Babylonia through paying tribute. Immense amounts of tribute supplemented the booty originating from the frequent campaigns, and helped the inhabitants of Babylonia to grow wealthy. The most visible effects of this affluence were spectacular public buildings, of which by far the most expensive was the reconstructed ziqqurrat of Babylon, best known as the Tower of Babel. Ninety by ninety meters square and about ninety meters high, it must have been the most massive structure ever built in ancient Mesopotamia (fig. 61). Its amazing height and the name Etemenanki, "House of the Bond

FIGURE 62. Bird's-eye view of the Ishtar Gate and the processional street, seen from the northwest (based on a painting by H. Anger). The "Tower of Babel" appears near the top right-hand corner.

between Heaven and Earth," led to the Old Testament story of divine punishment for a blasphemous attempt to reach heaven. The explanation for the confusion of tongues contained in the same narrative may be an allusion to the fact that more languages were spoken in sixth-century BCE Babylon than anywhere else. Babylon was certainly the metropolis of the time.

The ziqqurrat was but a part of an extensive temple complex dedicated to Marduk, the city god of Babylon who was also the highest of the Babylonian gods. The gathering place for New Year's festivities was a special temple outside the city. These festivities were considered essential for the well-being of the country, to the extent that the Assyrian kings, even in years of tension, ensured their celebration. A processional street paved with large stone slabs, flanked by walls decorated with molded, color-glazed tiles representing lions and composite animal figures, led from the temple of Marduk through the famous Ishtar Gate, as lavishly decorated as the walls, to the temple of the New Year (fig. 62).

Both the double city wall and the famous Hanging Gardens of Babylon within the palace compound were later counted among the seven wonders of the world. In its size and the height of the ceilings, the palace itself is no less impressive than the Assyrian palaces, though the walls are covered not with stone reliefs but with color-glazed tiles or wall paintings, which, however, have survived in fragments only.

Most other Babylonian cities were also generously embellished, and the main temples were both enlarged and beautified. The new wealth showed up in other respects too. At no time after the first centuries of the second millennium were so many new settlements founded or so many canals dug or extended. Whereas private dwellings had earlier been built of sun-dried mud brick, an entire neighborhood of private houses in Uruk was now built of baked bricks. The general prosperity was further reflected in many thousands of business documents. Yet another "first" was the founding of the Egibi family banking house in Babylon, with branches in Nippur and Uruk.

This period saw the unfolding of the sciences—albeit resting on older foundations—which reached a high point in the fifth and fourth centuries BCE. Mathematics has already been mentioned, as well as the ramifying genre of lists, or classification, which contributed to a clearer conception of the universe. The desire to foresee the future led to the compilation of observations from which predictions of good or bad events could be drawn. Astronomic observations, beyond their predictive role, provided a primer for scientific procedures in the strict sense, since mathematical methods had to be devised in order to calculate the course of celestial bodies. These Babylonian methods, which have stood the test of modern computation, found acceptance in both Greek astronomy and the Vedic astronomy of India. It was in Babylonia that the zodiac system originated. Babylonian medicine was presented in two handbooks of forty tablets each, organized according to therapeutic and diagnostic procedures. These texts deeply influenced both Greek medicine and the medicine of later periods in the Near East.

The unimpeded development of these fields was not matched by political development. After Nebuchadnezzar's reign, Babylon's years as an independent unit were numbered. Political decay was greatly accelerated by the enigmatic behavior of the usurper Nabonidus (555–539), who, after six years in Babylon, appointed his son Belshazzar governor of Babylon and retreated for ten years to the oasis settlement of Teima, at the northern fringes of the Arabian Peninsula. Why he did so remains unknown, though many of his contemporaries attempted to explain his actions. Nabonidus himself spoke of a surfeit of civilization; others claimed religious or military reasons. By 648 BCE, the Persian ruler Cyrus had already defeated the Medes and conquered all the territories east of the Tigris. After conquering southeastern Anatolia, Cyrus had added Lydia to his area by defeating its king, Croesus. The danger should have been obvious.

In 539 BCE, Nabonidus returned from Teima to Babylon, but it was too late, for the enemy forces were already marching toward his country. On September 14 of that year, Babylon was occupied without resistance, and on October 29, Cyrus entered the city in triumph. There is no clear information on the fate of Nabonidus. While some sources report his death, there are also hints that he was appointed governor of the south Iranian province of Carmania.

The quick disappearance of the Babylonian empire is less surprising than that of the Assyrian empire. Steady expansion over many centuries had enabled Assyria to accumulate experience in handling and administering very large territories. Babylonia, in contrast, had remained within narrow confines, at least from the middle of the second millennium. Furthermore, the main actors of the Chaldaean empire, who originated as tribal chiefs, had hardly any practical knowledge that might have prevented the immense territory inherited from the Assyrians from disintegrating. There was a conspicuous lack of any expansionist or even imperialistic ideology. Like the Assyrians, the Babylonians pillaged foreign countries and conducted wars simply to replenish their own resources. Under these circumstances, it must have been the extraordinary personalities of Nabopolassar and, Nebuchadnezzar that allowed the empire to survive as long as it did. When the weak ruler Nabonidus took over, the end was inevitable.

The formation of the Assyrian empire signified the emergence of a new kind of political organization. The gradual but accelerating process reminds us of the way the state under the Akkad dynasty emerged in the second half of the third millennium. In a constellation of similarly organized, almost equally sized political units, all the units were just strong enough to hold each other in check. Eventually, the constant and changing struggles for power resulted in the supremacy of one of the contenders, uniting the territories of the former adversaries and thus converting interstate problems into problems within the state. This slow development, repeatedly interrupted by stagnation or setbacks, helped shape the instruments that put Assyria, from the time of the large-scale expansions of the fourteenth and thirteenth centuries, in a position to meet most of the challenges faced by a great power. It is natural that the new structures were not perfect from the outset. While attempts were launched to develop a common infrastructure, like the establishment of a system of overland roads or the extension of settlements in foreign areas, Assyria's main concern was to strengthen its own country and to extract from foreign regions the necessary means. It was too early for the formulation of concepts such as decentralization or granting certain rights of autonomy, which subsequently helped the Achaemenids to avoid some of the problems suffered by the Assyrian empire.

8 The Achaemenid Empire (539–331 BCE)

Toward the end of the second millennium, the Assyrians had begun to extend their area of influence, looking especially at the eastern mountainous regions. After the mid-eighth century BCE, Tiglath-Pileser III, from one of the two dominant groups of this period, used the designation "Land of the Medes" for the area up to Mount Demavend in the east. Locating the Persians proves to be more difficult. From the ninth century on, we find repeated mentions of a land called Parsuash, or Parsumash, but in widely differing contexts, as if the land had moved from the northern to the southern Zagros. This confusion may be due to the Assyrians' uncertain geographical knowledge. Nevertheless, it tells us that the Persians were already counted among the more influential groups in the mountainous area. They were probably also among those groups creating organizational structures of their own in order to counterbalance Assyrian pressure. At the same time, they recognized Assyrian supremacy, since king Cyrus I of Parsumash sent ample tribute, and even one of his sons as a hostage, to Assurbanipal's court at Nineveh.

The Medes took the lead in the anti-Assyria coalition, which by the end of the seventh century, in conjunction with the Babylonians, had brought down the Assyrian power. The Persians had joined this coalition and had entered closer relations with the Medes through intermarriage. Soon, however, quarrels started between Cyrus II (559–530 BCE), the grandson of Cyrus I, founder of the dynasty, and Astyages, the Median father-in-law of Cyrus's father, Cambyses. Settling the conflict in his favor, Cyrus II reigned over the former Median territories as well as his own, and after

550 he also controlled the part of the former Assyrian empire that the Medes had received as booty.

Breaking with the way the Assyrian heritage had been divided, Cyrus set out to conquer Babylonia as well. After marching into Babylon in 539, he had himself crowned king of that city. With this move he extended his claim to the entire area that the Babylonians had inherited from the Assyrian empire. Only his death in 530, during a campaign against nomadic tribes in the northeast of his realm, prevented him from achieving that ambition.

Cyrus is said to have been received in Babylon as a liberator—at least that is how it is described in contemporary sources, whose main intention seems to have been to undermine the government of Nabonidus by indicating that the foreign invader was more acceptable than the incumbent. The unusual mercy that Cyrus had shown during his conquests in Asia Minor, and his strategy of not interfering in religious matters, a policy he upheld in Babylonia too, may have become well known. He is famous for releasing the Jews from the Babylonian captivity. In spite of this release, a large Jewish community remained in Babylon, lively enough to develop the multivolume Babylonian Talmud several hundred years later.

Mesopotamia now became marginal to the main scene in the Near East. The core area was Persis, the original home of the Persians, corresponding to the modern Iranian province of Fars. All the Persian capitals and main royal residences—Pasargadae, Persepolis, Egbatana (today's Hamadan) and Susa—were located on Iranian soil. While the year 539 BCE signified a break in the territorial political continuity, numerous surviving business documents show that Babylonia remained the economic center. In spite of heavy Aramaic influence, such documents continued to be written predominantly in Babylonian cuneiform. The only visible change was the new dating system: years were now counted according to the years in office of the new rulers. No signs of any interruption or insecurity have been found with respect to business conducted in Babylon, Nippur, and Uruk; to events concerning the temple employees of the residential area of Uruk or the common merchants in Babylon; to sales and real estate contracts; or to money transactions. Even the banking houses of Egibi and Murashu continued working as if nothing had happened—remarkable

FIGURE 63. Extension of the Achaemenid empire at the time of Darius I, ca. 500 BCE

in light of the known sensitivity of the money markets. Babylon continued to be the metropolis.

Cyrus's claim to the entire territory formerly under Babylonian control was followed up by his son Cambyses II, who, only four years after his ascent to the throne, defeated the Egyptian army at Pelusium and thus made Egypt part of his realm (fig. 63).

What followed was the first of a long series of hereditary conflicts within the ruling family, which finally proved instrumental in the fall of the Achaemenid empire. On his return from Egypt, Cambyses died under obscure circumstances. His successor, Darius I (521–486 BCE), relates in a lengthy rock inscription at Bisutun (see fig. 66 below) that prior to the Egyptian campaign Cambyses had had his brother Smerdis killed; he had been forced to return prematurely from Egypt because the magician Gaumata had posed as Smerdis with the idea of seizing the throne. Darius, by then king, had prevented the usurpation by killing Gaumata. The apologetic tone of the inscription, plus the fact that Darius—as a member of a collateral line of the ruling Achaemenid family—had to defend himself against a revolt of numerous local rulers, suggests that even in his own time Darius was suspected of complicity in the murder of Smerdis, and may not have been totally innocent in the death of Cambyses either.

Nonetheless, Darius grew to be one of the most influential figures of his age. During the thirty-five years of his reign, he sponsored numerous innovations, including a common official

FIGURE 64. Architectural remains on the terrace of Persepolis

language and a common monetary system. He followed the Assyrian example by dividing his realm into provinces and building a far-flung system of overland roads. With the palace of Susa and the palatial terrace of Persepolis he created magnificent examples of Near Eastern architecture (figs. 64 and 65). Architectural elements such as the column and the pillared hall were introduced, while walls covered with sculptured stone slabs or reliefs made of color-glazed tiles are reminiscent of models in Nineveh and Babylon.

The inscription on a rock face near Bisutun, mentioned above, which overlooks the old (and modern) main highway between Babylon and Hamadan, has gained a special importance in Near Eastern studies because the text is repeated in three languages: Elamite, Babylonian, and Old Persian (fig. 66). The Old Persian part used a newly created, specifically Persian cuneiform. In the early nineteenth century CE, the trilingual text served as the basic material for deciphering the cuneiform writing system.

In introducing a common official language, Darius took advantage of the fact that Aramaic dialects had previously been spoken and written throughout fairly large parts of his territory. Standardization resulted in the emergence of "Imperial Aramaic," used for documents found in regions ranging from Egypt to India.

The general calmness prevailing under Darius did not prevent Babylon's repeated attempts to regain its independence. In 522

FIGURE 65. Glazed brick relief representing a guard at the palace of Darius at Susa

FIGURE 66. Darius's relief on a rockface at Bisutun, with trilingual inscriptions on the smooth surfaces below

and 521 BCE, two usurpers, Nebuchadnezzar III and Nebuchadnezzar IV, exploited the turmoil at the death of Cambyses II to establish an independent reign of their own, but they were swiftly deposed by Darius.

A more serious revolt began in Babylonia in 479 but was bloodily suppressed by Xerxes (485–465 BCE). According to Herodotus, it entailed the destruction of the "temple of Zeus," that is, the temple of Markuk (probably the temple complex of Esagila). Herodotus also reports that Xerxes had ordered the golden statue of the god to be melted down and the "tomb of Belus" (Herodotus's designation for the ziqqurrat Etemenanki) to be destroyed. But this destruction by Xerxes did not mark the end of the cult of Marduk. Cuneiform documents indicate that it was kept alive until the end of the Achaemenid period.

Two other places in Mesopotamia gained military importance during this period. The first was Kunaxa, probably not far from modern Baghdad, which acquired literary fame for a battle fought there. During the armed conflict between Artaxerxes II (404–359) and his brother Cyrus, the satrap of Sardes, Cyrus had recruited a large contingent of Greek mercenaries. After the battle was lost, one of the generals by the name of Xenophon led the Greeks on their return march to the coast of the Black Sea and gave a vivid report in his "Anabasis." The second place was Gaugamela, probably somewhere east of Mosul but not fully identified. It was here that Alexander won the last and decisive battle against Darius III and his Persian army, marking the end of serious resistance and allowing Alexander to regard himself as the legitimate heir of the entire former Achaemenid empire. Darius escaped eastward, hoping that Bessos, the satrap of Baktria, would give him shelter and protection. He was murdered on arrival, however, obviously in anticipation that his death would ease relations with the conqueror.

Thus ended the period of the Achaemenid supremacy, which had united an immense territory. Experiences from earlier periods had been used to ensure its control and governability. Innovations including a common official language and script, a common monetary system, and an extended road system with way stations all became integral elements of the empires to come. Partial decentralization, combined with the substantial independence of the satrapies—a reaction to the strict centralization of the Assyrians—was less successful because of the ambition and aggressiveness of various family members. In the end, dimensions proved too large for the conflicts to be solved on the level of family problems.

After the dissolution of both the political and military power of Assyria, this northern part of Mesopotamia played a relatively minor role in the surrounding regions for quite a long time. Life in Babylonia, on the other hand, went on as usual; only the political figures changed. Babylon had ceased to be the political center, but—in contrast to the Iranian core area—it clearly remained the cultural and economic metropolis of the entire Near East.

9 Alexander and the Seleucids in Babylonia

(331–141 BCE)

After his decisive victory at Gaugamela in 331 BCE, Alexander turned to Babylon, where, according to several sources, he was greeted by officials, priests, and the populace even before reaching the city gate. Cuneiform sources call him "King of all Regions," a title used by the Achaemenid kings. He decreed the rebuilding of the temple of Marduk and installed a new administration. Leaving a Macedonian garrison in Babylon, Alexander continued marching toward Susa and Persepolis, arriving at the latter city on February 1, 330 BCE. Only after the burning of Persepolis—it still is unsolved whether it was accidental or intended—did he set out to conquer the regions farther east.

Several reports indicate that Alexander became increasingly "orientalized" during his march to the Indus. He not only grew fond of the lifestyle he was encountering but also liked the way local potentates behaved and were treated. For instance, he so much identified himself as the legitimate heir to the Persian kings that he avenged the murder of Darius by ordering the execution of Darius's murderer, Bessos. Alexander wanted to assume for himself a custom of the Achaemenid kings that Xenophon had described as disgusting—the people's prostration before the king as sign of submission—but his wish was not granted. Another example of his adopting oriental customs was the mass wedding in Susa, where, in addition to himself and his close entourage, ninety of his Macedonian army officers were married to Persian women, symbolizing the integration of the two cultures.

From the outset, Alexander seems to have intended an important role for Babylon or for the whole of Babylonia. Thus, instead

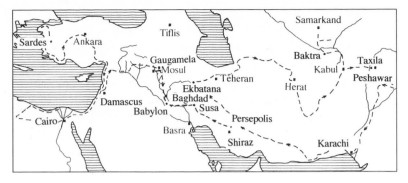

FIGURE 67. Route of Alexander's expedition

of pursuing Darius after his victory at Gaugamela, he immediately veered south toward Babylon, demonstrating his interest in this city. After completing his eastern campaigns, he returned to Babylon in 323 BCE, taking up residence in the westernmost part of Nebuchadnezzar's main palace, a bastion protruding into the Tigris. For the following months, contemporary sources mention a projected reconnaissance trip down the Euphrates and a plan to conquer the Arabian Peninsula. None of this happened, however, as Alexander died on June 10, 323 BCE, in the palace in Babylon.

There is no question that Alexander's campaigns and the foundation of numerous cities where Greeks were left as residents laid the foundation for the encompassing change known as Hellenization. But this change did not occur overnight; nor did it occur everywhere simultaneously or with equal effect. Initially, Hellenization touched only a small section of the local upper class.

When Alexander died, his son had not yet been born. Since no direct dynastic succession was possible, Alexander's half-brother Arrhidaeus was made king under the throne name of Philip. Who should actually wield power, however, was a matter of dispute among the *diadokhai,* the generals who had held high rank in Alexander's army. These struggles ended with Antigonos Monophthalmos ("the one-eyed") proving to be the strongest. His realm encompassed mainly the eastern parts of the former empire.

In 321 BCE, Seleucus, another former military commander in Alexander's army, was appointed satrap of Babylon. Following a dispute with Antigonos, he saw fit to escape to Egypt, and only the victory at Gaza of the *diadokhai,* who had combined forces against Antigonos in 312, enabled Seleucus to return to Babylon. In several subsequent campaigns, he expanded his sphere of influence to include Syria and Asia Minor. In the long run, this expansion had fatal consequences for Babylonia, for the seat of political power shifted to the west, resulting in the foundation of a new capital, Antiokhia (now Antakya), on the Orontes River in 300 BCE. Not long before, Seleucus had founded the city of Seleucia on the western banks of the Tigris, thirty-five kilometers south of modern Baghdad, with the intention of bringing commerce and population there from the city of Babylon. Despite these activities, Babylon retained its importance and itself came under Hellenistic influence, as witnessed by the remains of a Greek theater.

Philip Arrhidaeus, having succeeded Alexander in Babylon, was the first to introduce a calendar that counted years from a fixed date rather than from the first year of a king's reign and was thus supposed to last forever—another innovation. Because of Alexander's historical importance, already recognized at that time, the date of his death, June 10, 323 BCE, was taken as the first day of the new era. For personal and political reasons, the calendar was revised shortly after its introduction: Seleucus I—who in the meantime had adopted the epithet *nicator,* meaning "victor"—decreed that the date of his return from Egypt to Babylon on October 1, 312 BCE, should be the first day. This dating system, known as the Seleucid era, lasted a long time and was used in Jewish literature well into the eleventh century CE, when it was replaced by a system still in use today that counts years from the supposed creation of the world on October 7, 3761 BCE.

In 293 BCE, Seleucus appointed as co-regent his son Antiochus I, who acquired the epithet *soter,* "the savior." After retaining Seleucia on the Tigris as his official seat for the first few years of his reign, he moved to Antiokhia after his father's death in 281, reigning from there until 261. These years saw the composition of a substantial historical work on Babylonia, written in Greek. The author, Berossos, was a priest of Marduk from Babylon who, out of loyalty to Seleucus, had accompanied him westward when he fled from Antigonos. Having lived on the Greek island of Kos for some years, Berossos had become fluent in Greek. His three-volume

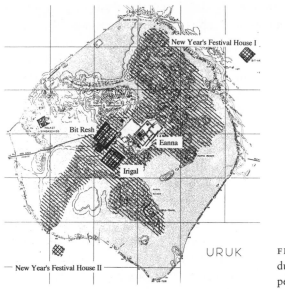

URUK

FIGURE 68. Uruk
during the Seleucid
period, ca. 200 BCE

Babyloniaka is a comprehensive history of Babylonia from primeval times to Alexander's rule. Presumably the work was written to acquaint Antiochus I with the history of the region and, in addition, to allow him to identify himself with this history and to view himself as the legitimate successor of the Babylonian rulers.

Several wars were fought with the Egyptian Ptolemies over the borders in Syria, and later military campaigns tried in vain to retain the eastern possessions of the empire. None of this action touched Babylonia, whose internal development is substantiated by numerous cuneiform texts. On the one hand we see that Hellenization was encouraged—for example by the foundation of Seleucia. On the other hand we observe an unprecedented revitalization of Babylonian culture. Not only are there many references to the unimpaired continuation of the cults of the traditional Babylonian gods and to the copying of old cultic texts, but, even more significant, we know that new complexes were being built in the best tradition of Babylonian architecture.

The huge terrace in the western part of Uruk, which shortly before 3000 BCE had swallowed up the White Temple, had repeatedly served as a foundation for new buildings that are known only from written sources. Lower levels were overlaid, and thus unexcavatable, by a massive architectural complex called Bit Resh, "main temple." This complex was built by the local governor Anu-uballit Nikarchos in 244 BCE, and enlarged in 202 BCE by Anu-uballit Kephalon. Bit Resh is mentioned for the last time in 139 BCE. Both governors had good Babylonian names supplemented by Greek epithets.

In every detail the plan of Bit Resh follows the ancient Near Eastern tradition and could just as well have been built 250 years earlier. It was dedicated to Anu, the Babylonian god of heaven, and his consort Antum. The southeastern part was badly damaged by excavations in the nineteenth century CE, which uncovered numerous cuneiform tablets containing hymns, prayers, lamentations, and rituals written in Sumerian interlined with a Babylonian translation. They are copies of older texts, written in Seleucid times. In many cases, ancient Sumerian cultic texts are known only because of these copies. The tablets had probably belonged to an extensive temple library, where they were both written and stored. Apparently the scribal school attached to the library was charged with providing texts for daily use in the cult, but the tablets were also part of an endeavor to collect the literature of earlier periods and to preserve it by copying—much as was done by Assurbanipal.

Single tablets found in the complex of Irigal, south of Bit Resh but scarcely explored, dating to approximately 200 BCE, point to a similar context. The idea of preserving older works of literature, however, is not restricted to these temples, for a similar archive was found in Uruk in the house of a priest, and few tablets were even found in private homes.

The Babylonian character of Seleucid Uruk can also be observed at numerous other sites. For instance, the traditional Babylonian main temple, the Eanna-ziqqurrat, was repaired in that period, and outside of the city wall a large complex for the Babylonian New Year's festival was erected on previously open land.

This emphasis on reviving Babylonian traditions may also apply to other cities, though evidence is sparse. From Babylon itself we have found copies of the same kinds of texts as those from Uruk, as well as numerous business documents in Babylonian cuneiform, which testify to a strong Babylonian component. On the other hand, we have found remains not only of a Greek theater in Babylon but also of Attic black-figured vases; and the presence of stamped handles of amphoras shows that wine from Rhodes was shipped to Babylon. Contrary to Seleucus's intention, not everything was moved from Babylon to Seleucia. It was not until 275 BCE, still under Antiochus I, that part of the population of Babylon was relocated to Seleucia.

As an intentionally Hellenistic city, Seleucia was not affected by the revival of Babylonian culture. The rectangular grid of the streets clearly speaks for its Greek origin. Within a very short period it became a center of commerce with a population of six hundred thousand.

Toward the end of the reign of Antiochus III (223–187 BCE), a new satrapy, On the Red Sea, was carved out from the southern part of the Babylonia satrapy for unknown reasons. At that time the name Red Sea was used for both for the Arabian Sea and the two gulfs today known as the Persian Gulf and the Red Sea. The territory of the new satrapy anticipated that of the kingdom of Characene in the subsequent Parthian period. We do not know whether Uruk already belonged to it.

In the first half of the second century BCE, the Parthian state, as a new power, began expanding from eastern Iran toward the west. Mithridates I (171–139 BCE) was proclaimed king in Seleucia. In 139, Antiochus VII, a member of the former ruling family, was able to reconquer Babylonia for a short period. His death in 129 during conflicts in Media meant the final expulsion of the Seleucids from their eastern possessions and their restriction to the Syrian and east Anatolian region.

10 The Empires of the Parthians and the Sasanians (141 BCE to 642 CE)

The Parthian king Phraates II (138–128 BCE) in 129 regained supremacy over Babylonia, which had been lost ten years earlier to the Seleucid ruler Antiochus VII. From this year until the end of the Sasanian period, the imperial capital was Ctesiphon, on the eastern side of the Tigris, across from Seleucia. Prior to embarking on a lengthy campaign toward the east, Phraates appointed Himeros from Hyrkania (region south of the Caspian) vice-regent of Babylon. Himeros punished the Babylonian cities for their role in the Seleucids' regaining power; the burning of the great Seleucid temple complexes in Uruk was probably part of this action.

The unclear distribution of power at the end of the Seleucid interlude presented a good climate for marginal areas of the empire to break off. In the southern part of Babylonia, in the vicinity of the new satrapy On the Red Sea, a petty state emerged with Charax as its capital, on the banks of the Shatt el-Arab, not far from today's Khorramshahr. In 130 BCE a certain Hyspaosines started minting coins of his own and expanding his territory northward. Similar coins found in Uruk and in Tello (the third-millennium city of Girsu) may indicate that these cities temporarily have marked the northern limits. But Hyspaosines apparently had wider ambitions, for in 127 BCE we encounter him as king of Babylon—soon to be expelled, however, by the Parthian king Artabanos II (128–124 BCE). Hyspaosines died in 124, but coins continue to be minted until 121, indicating that his territory managed to retain some significance even after the death of its founder.

Mithridates II (123–88 BCE) waged far-reaching campaigns, both to secure existing possessions and to conquer new ones. His

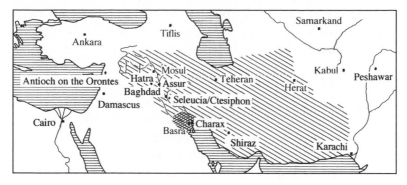

FIGURE 69. Extension of the Parthian empire, first century BCE

campaigns were directed primarily against the remains of the Seleucid state in the northwest but also against the eastern regions. Since Mesopotamia was considered a militarily pacified region, it was hardly mentioned in written sources. A hoard of coins minted in Nineveh and found there suggests that the old Assyrian capital had regained some importance.

Seleucia had finally inherited Babylon's status as metropolis and commercial center. Its importance increased further when, during a visit from a delegation of the Chinese Han Dynasty in 115 BCE, it was agreed to open a trade route that would link China and the Mediterranean. Seleucia was favorably located since it not only lay on the Tigris but was fairly close to one of the very few roads leading to a pass across the Zagros Mountains. This road subsequently became a part of a branch of the "Silk Road"; it corresponds to the modern route between Teheran and Baghdad, passing through Hamadan and Kermanshah.

In other parts of Babylonia, especially in the south, the irrigation systems decayed, and the population became noticeably impoverished. In Uruk, for instance, primitive sheds were built into the ruins of the Seleucid complexes. Another sign of the region's reduced circumstances was the absence of coins, which with very few exceptions reappeared only in the middle of the first century CE. Substantial finds of coins from the time of Gotarzes II (38–51 CE) speak for a rapidly expanding settlement, soon to extend over the whole of Babylonia.

These 130-odd years must have seen important changes, though we have hardly any records. When in the fourth decade of the first century CE we see the revival of large-scale building and settlement, we recognize a widespread Hellenistic orientation even outside the cities.

Mithridates I had set a programmatic emphasis with far-reaching consequences for his successors by accepting the epithet *philhellen*, "friend of the Greeks." During the Seleucid period, Hellenistic influences had reached only a small number of non-Greeks, who entertained close relations with the newly founded Hellenistic cities. It was not until Parthian times, in the first centuries CE, that Hellenization was achieved on a grand scale, evident in architectural forms and decoration, in the numerous terracotta figurines in Greek dress, and in the demise of most traditional Babylonian cults. In Babylon, the cult of Marduk in the main temple area of Esagila is no longer mentioned after the first century CE; in Nippur, the main temple complex including the ziqqurrat was converted into a fortification; and in Uruk, Parthian soldiers hacked out a lookout space for themselves in the tower of the Eanna ziqqurrat.

From the mid-first century on, the settled area of the city of Uruk was far bigger than it had been at any time since the beginning of the third millennium. Almost the entire area within the confines of the old city wall shows remains of this period. Following an ancient tradition, private houses, often quite spacious, were arranged around a central courtyard. In some, a long gallery, entirely open at one end, gave onto the courtyard. Usually vaulted in later times, this architectural component, known as a liwan, was apparently used for the first time in the Parthian period but soon proliferated. It became one of the most characteristic features in Sasanian and, more particularly, Islamic architecture. In addition to the use of mud plaster, houses were finished with a heavy coat of stucco, into which Hellenistic design elements had been cut.

In the southern part of Uruk, a small temple is still standing, originally within an extended fortification complex. According to an inscription, it was dedicated to an otherwise unknown god, Gareus, certainly not one of the local pantheon. Still, the temple clearly included ancient Near Eastern elements: for example, a cella, separated from the main interior space by two short walls, and a niche in the rear wall for a cult image. In contrast, the facade is structured according to Hellenistic principles, with pilasters and arches. The building faced a colonnaded street, another Hellenistic element of architecture.

The countryside, unlike its earlier character, was now covered by a large number of rural settlements. This growth is particularly striking for the southern part of Babylonia, for few permanent settlements had existed outside of the major cities since the occupation by Aramaic and Chaldaean tribes. This resettlement happened in so short a time that we are compelled to look for a specific reason. Lacking firm evidence, we can only guess that the Euphrates had assumed a new role, accompanied by a massive overhaul of the irrigation systems or even the construction of new canals.

The Euphrates had become part of an international trade route linking India and the Roman Empire. Goods from India were unloaded in Charax and reloaded onto river craft, which were towed up the Euphrates. Near Dura Europos on the Syrian Euphrates, a fortified settlement founded by Macedonians at the end of the third century BCE, the goods were moved to Palmyra, an oasis on the trade route, and transported from there to the Mediterranean coast. Palmyrean and Greek merchants who had established trade stations in Charax carried on most of the trade. A tombstone found in Uruk with the epitaph of a Greek merchant who died there in III CE testifies to this involvement.

To guarantee the necessary water level, the embankments of the Euphrates had to be constantly maintained, since they were liable to be damaged by the annual floods. At the same time, securing the dams was a prerequisite for the proper functioning of the irrigation canals, which were fed mainly by the Euphrates. The ensuing high agricultural yields were probably what prompted Pliny the Elder in the first century CE, in his *Naturalis historia,* to describe Babylonia as "ager totius orientis fertilissimus," "the most fertile land in the entire Orient."

Babylonia was only marginally affected by the constant battles of the Parthian rulers with rebellious groups in the eastern provinces, or the disputes with the Roman Empire over the question whether the Syrian Euphrates should serve as the demarcation line between the Parthian and the Roman spheres of influence. An exception was the campaign of the Roman emperor Trajan during the years 114–117 CE. Trajan's original idea was to settle the dispute over the possession of Armenia, but he then marched southward along the Euphrates, conquered Ctesiphon in 116 CE, and converted Babylonia into the Roman province of "Assyria." As a reward for this military achievement, the Roman senate endowed him with the title "Parthicus." Symbolizing the subjugation of the entire region, Trajan stuck his sword into the "Lower Sea," that is, the Persian Gulf. The vassal state, whose capital was Charax, was spared, for it was the end of the trade route that passed through Palmyra, so important for the Romans. Securing this route was undoubtedly one of the main incentives for the conquest of Babylonia.

Revolts in northern Mesopotamia, especially a futile siege of Hatra, prompted Trajan to withdraw to Syria in 117 CE. He died while planning a new campaign against Babylonia. Trajan's successor, Hadrian, abandoned such plans, and was willing to renew recognition of the Syrian Euphrates as the border, an agreement sealed in a meeting between himself and the Parthian ruler Osroes in 123 CE.

With the exception of isolated pieces of information like the hoard of coins found in Nineveh, mentioned above, we hear next to nothing about northern Mesopotamia. Being minted in that city, the coins do reveal that Nineveh was not a backwater. Furthermore, major construction works in the old capital of Assur and in the city of Hatra in the western steppe during the Parthian period show that northern Mesopotamia was more widely inhabited than suggested by the written sources. As in the south, the recovery began only in the first century CE. Assur had become the seat of a local administration, which certainly provided the impetus for development around it. In contrast to the south, where the old cults had been ousted, the cult of the god Assur was continued in the city Assur, though the temple's architecture was now in the liwan style.

An extensive palace constructed over the demolished city wall of old Assur, close to the Tigris, contained several new architectural forms. Liwans opened onto all four sides of an internal courtyard. In Hellenistic style, the facades around the courtyard were formed by triple rows of superimposed columns. During the destruction,

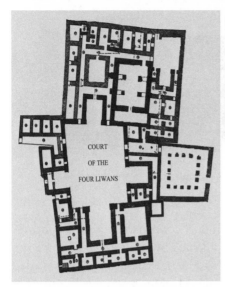

COURT
OF THE
FOUR LIWANS

FIGURE 70. Plan of
the Parthian palace
at Assur, first century
CE, and its facades

one of these stuccoed facades had fallen into the courtyard, virtually in one piece; it was totally retrieved and is now exhibited in Berlin's Near Eastern Museum.

Also reflecting Hellenistic architecture was a large courtyard surrounded by colonnaded galleries. Unlike any known form, however, was an almost square, free-standing cube of ten by twelve meters, with a single entrance, fit into a larger square, leaving a corridor only two meters wide between the walls. Access to this corridor was equally limited. The inner space and corridor probably served a specific purpose, perhaps ritual.

Private houses of this period likewise exhibited a mixture of ancient Near Eastern tradition (arrangement around a central courtyard), Hellenistic influence (architectural ornamentation), and Parthian innovation (the liwan).

This fusion of elements becomes conspicuous in the city of Hatra, sixty kilometers west of Assur in the steppe area. In the mid-second century CE, a first-century BCE Aramaic settlement was enlarged and converted into a fortified round city with a diameter of two kilometers. In 166 CE, Hatra became the capital of a small realm whose rulers called themselves kings of the Arabs.

FIGURE 71. Side-by-side liwans in the temple complex in Hatra (1966 photograph)

The inhabitants of the steppe areas between the middle Euphrates and the Tigris had been called Arabs by the Assyrians since the ninth century BCE. The center of Hatra was occupied by a walled temple complex in which the sun god was worshiped. The vaulted ceilings of the four liwans, constructed with ashlars, have been preserved in part. Built of stone rather than the usual mud brick, the ruin creates a monumental impression, even today (fig. 71).

Particularly impressive is the rich sculptural decoration, in most cases firmly attached to the architecture. Both on the facades and in the interior of the halls, human masks look down from the walls, carved as reliefs on some of the ashlars. A number of consoles at varying heights, similarly worked from ashlars, indicate that they once served as bases for statues. Indeed, numerous statues have been found on the ground, of which many had been used for embellishing the walls, though the taller ones may have been set up somewhere within the large halls.

The statues themselves illustrate a mixture of Hellenistic and local elements. While their clothing, with puffed robes and long trousers, represents the local fashion of the day, its execution, with folds and layering, clearly follows Hellenistic examples (fig. 72). We find men and women belonging to the local hierarchy but also Hellenistic heroes like Heracles. The ubiquitous inscriptions are written in a local Aramaic dialect, which was also the language of the proper names of the rulers and very likely the mother tongue of the majority. On the other hand, a number of Arabic names bear

FIGURE 72. Statue of a king, from Hatra
(height: 197 cm)

witness to the arrival of the final wave of the Semitic groups that
had reached Mesopotamia from the Arabian Peninsula.

Built onto the rear wall of one of the liwans in Hatra, we find
an architectural element resembling the enigmatic square chamber
in the Parthian palace of Assur, again a cube of sixteen by sixteen
meters, surrounded by a corridor four and one-half meters wide.
This stone structure, preserved to a height of fourteen meters,
gives an even stronger impression of confinement and was almost
certainly connected to some kind of ritual.

One almost pure example of Hellenistic influence was found in
Hatra: a Roman temple with a colonnade, erected on a raised terrace. This structure is especially striking, since a thorough mixture
of styles characterizes everything else.

Following a lull in conflicts with the Romans, Vologases IV
(148–192 CE) took advantage of the death of the Roman emperor
Antonius Pius in 161 CE to wage a war. From 162 on, the Romans
started counterattacking. In 166, a military commander of the
Roman emperor Marcus Aurelius conquered Seleucia, leading to

the destruction of the palace of the Parthian capital Ctesiphon. The Roman army was forced to retreat because of an outbreak of plague, but in spite of the recovery of Parthian rule, the Euphrates ceased to form the Parthian border, which instead was moved to the more eastern tributary, the river Habur. The principal casualty of these wars was the trade route from Palmyra down the Euphrates to Charax. Because undisturbed trade benefited both parties, and because the Romans had serious problems in other parts of the empire, the Parthians and the Romans apparently agreed on some kind of armistice, which lasted for two decades.

After 195 CE, clashes began again. An attack by Vologases V (192–207) on the Syrian city of Nisibis, which was under Roman control, provoked a counterattack by the Roman emperor Septimius Severus, who took Seleucia and Babylon in 196 and destroyed Ctesiphon yet again. On the return march, the Roman army besieged Hatra twice, both times without success.

In addition to power struggles between Vologases VI (207–226) and his brother Artabanos IV (213–224), who ruled with him for a while, continuing clashes with Roman armies, along with the difficulty of keeping vassal contingents under control, so weakened Parthian power that the Parthians could put up little resistance to the revolt of their vassal prince of Istakhr in the province of Persis. Ardashir I (227–241), who was the son of the local ruler Papak, started to expand his territory after 220. His aspiration to comprehensive rule was manifested by his founding of a new city. Gur (now Firuzabad), in the southern part of the modern province of Fars, was designed as a circular city with a palace at its center.

In 224, the Parthian ruler Artabanos IV was defeated in Media, and Ctesiphon was conquered in 226. That same year, Ardashir I had himself crowned in Ctesiphon as "King of Kings," the old title of the Achaemenid rulers. Though failing to conquer Hatra in 227, by 230 he had managed to assemble under his rule almost all of the former Parthian territory.

Ardashir's actions opened a new chapter for Mesopotamia. Both Parthians and Sasanians—as the new rulers called themselves after an ancestor called Sasan—had their roots in Iran. Owing to the openness of the Parthian rulers to Hellenism, their geopolitical center was located in the western part of their realm rather than in Iran. Though again ruling from Ctesiphon as their capital, Ardashir and his successors deliberately kept their center of gravity in Iran. More emphatically than the Parthians, they claimed to be the heirs of the Achaemenids deriving legitimacy for that claim from their ancestral city of Istakhr. The city lay almost in the shadow of the huge terrace of Persepolis, which even as a ruin still dominated its surroundings. Within its range of visibility was the long rock face of what is now known as Naqsh-e Rustam, with the monumental tombs of the Achaemenid kings. No wonder the Sasanians too chose this site as their burial place.

There is little information on Mesopotamia for the following years. Being a possession, it was never endangered and thus was hardly ever mentioned in official or narrative accounts, which usually focused on conflicts or military campaigns.The land around Uruk in the southern part of Babylonia was undergoing a rapid decline. The only coins that have been found there date to Ardashir's early years; none are from his later years or from the reigns of his successors.

The lower Euphrates was losing importance as part of the trade route. Connections between China or India and the Mediterranean had started to shift. Not only had the trade route via the Euphrates been impaired by clashes between Parthians and Romans, but the Romans wanted to establish direct contacts with their trade partners. Thus they favored a northern route to China through southern Russia and Mongolia, and a southern route to India via the Red Sea and circumventing the Arabian Peninsula.

Ironically, Ardashir himself had contributed to this change by a decision apparently implemented early in his reign. In order to curb the influence of the Rome-friendly Palmyreans and to profit from increasing tariffs, Ardashir prevented Roman and Palmyrean ships from taking the direct route to Charax via the lower Euphrates. Instead, they were forced to use a canal that led them across to the Tigris, bringing them to Vologesias, Ctesiphon's warehouse. There, goods had to be transferred to other ships, which involved the imposition of fees. Whereas the incorporation of the Euphrates as part of an important trade route during the first century CE had entailed revitalizing the irrigation systems and resettling the countryside, recent neglect of the river caused the canal systems to decay and the southern Babylonian settlements to die.

As in earlier periods, neglecting the embankments had caused the Euphrates to shift to a new bed farther west, making use of the depressions close to the modern cities Najaf and Kufa. What little water remained in the old bed sufficed only for northern and central Babylonia. Things had become particularly precarious by the beginning of the third century CE because a new city was founded on the banks of the new river course. Hira, as the city was named, soon became a center of local power, and from the fourth century onward served as capital of the Sasanian vassal state of the Lakhmides. Restoring the conditions associated with the earlier course of the river was unthinkable.

The flowering of the state of the Lakhmides during the fifth and sixth centuries boosted southern Babylonia when a major canal was dug, connecting the Hira-Euphrates with the old course. Military camps, like small Roman forts with a rectangular layout, were established along the southern shore of the canal for reasons we can only guess at: fortifying Hira's southern border may have been a precautionary measure against the inhabitants of the Arabian Peninsula.

While southern Babylonia seems to have been more or less abandoned, the settling of northern and central Babylonia from the fifth century on was intensified by the establishment of a dense network of canals. The many parallel canals suggest an important change in irrigation technique. Until that time, all available water had been used for irrigation, causing the salt content of the soil to increase and sometimes leading to total infertility. The only remedy of any effectiveness, washing out the salts by a drainage system, may have been exercised here for the first time.

The excellent economic situation permitted a rich intellectual life, best known for of its religious components. Mani, the founder of a religion combining Zoroastrian and Christian elements, which soon had followers from Egypt to Central Asia, was born not far from Ctesiphon. After 242, we find him at the Sasanian court of Shapur I in Gundeshapur. Under Bahram I (273–276), however, he fell victim to the religious zeal of the high priest Karder, who succeeded in making Zoroastrianism the state religion, with con-

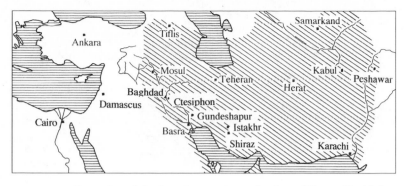

FIGURE 73. Extension of the Sasanian empire at the time of Shapur II, third century CE

comitant persecution of Christians and Manichaeans. Mani died in 276 in the prison at Gundeshapur.

Gundeshapur, which lies close to Susa in Khuzestan, was founded by Shapur I around 260 and populated with craftsmen brought in from Syria and with Roman prisoners of war. After the establishment of a university, the city soon became a cultural center. The university consisted of faculties for medicine, with a hospital attached; for theology; and for astronomy, with an observatory. In 484, Gundeshapur was the venue of a Christian council, in the course of which the Persian church settled on the Nestorian doctrine as their base. From then on, Nestorianism was standard for the entire area of the Sasanian Empire, including Mesopotamia and its numerous Christian dioceses and parishes. In Mesopotamia, Ctesiphon and Hira were selected as bishoprics.

Of major importance was the most comprehensive representation of Jewish religious erudition, the "Babylonian Talmud," mentioned in chapter 8 above. It took canonical shape between the fifth and the seventh centuries in the rabbinical academies of Babylonia.

As for northern Mesopotamia, no more is known for the Sasanian period than for the preceding centuries. Our main sources tell of military encounters, most importantly the conquest of Hatra by Shapur I in 241. Other areas are mentioned only occasionally. We only know that Shapur II (309–379) relocated large contingents of people from Istakhr and Isfahan to Nisibis and Kerkuk.

FIGURE 74. Main facade of the palace of Chosroes I in Ctesiphon. The photograph was taken by Robert Koldewey before the earthquake of 1872, when the right-hand part was still standing.

There are references to Zoroastrian fire temples in Erbil and elsewhere, and after the beginning of the fourth century we learn of the founding of many Christian churches and convents. Dioceses were established in Nisibis, Erbil, and Kerkuk during a Christian synod in Ctesiphon in 410. Notably, the separation of the Nestorian Christian church from the West and its consolidation in the Sasanian Empire had been encouraged by the expulsion of Nestorian scholars and theologians from (Roman) Edessa to (Sasanian) Nisibis, decreed by the Byzantine emperor Zeno.

The long and frequent struggles between the Sasanians and the East Roman (or Byzantine) Empire had always ended in a stalemate, with both adversaries waiting for favorable conditions to change the balance of power. In view of the turmoil regarding the succession in the East Roman Empire not long after 600, the Sasanian ruler Chosroes II (590–628) saw the opportunity for a war. Within a few years he succeeded in bringing under his control all of Syria as far as Jerusalem, as well as Asia Minor. In 615 he was at the gates of Constantinople, and even managed to conquer Egypt in 619. Giddy with success, he declined a peace offer by the new Byzantine emperor Heraclius, who had ascended the throne in 610. Chosroes was so sure that he could take Constantinople that he allowed Heraclius to advance toward Persia via Armenia. When in 626, however, Chosroes failed to take Constantinople after a long siege, Heraclius had already advanced deep into Sasanian territory, and in 627 he defeated the Sasanian army near Nineveh. A revolt led by Chosroes' son Sheroes resulted in the dismissal and subsequent death of Chosroes.

Soon afterward, an agreement was reached with the Byzantine Empire whereby the Sasanians would retreat to their former borders, those of 600 CE. Internally, however, the Sasanian Empire enjoyed no peace. Continuing struggles for succession resulted in five rulers' mounting the throne within a mere six years. When sixteen-year-old Yazdegerd III (632–651), one of Chosroes' grandsons, established himself on the throne, a religious and cultural phenomenon had started to gain momentum that even a more experienced ruler could not have controlled. In 622 the prophet Mohammed had left Mecca for Medina, and it was not long before an army was formed which, under the flag of the new religion, Islam, started moving northeast. Bahrain was conquered in 629, and its governor converted to Islam. Hira fell in 633, and in 634 the caliph Omar I called upon Yazdegerd to convert likewise. Yazdegerd's refusal prompted continuation of the conflicts. In 636, the Arabian and the Sasanian armies faced each other at Qadisiyah, southwest of Hira. Following the Arabs' victory, it did not take more than a couple of years for the Arabian forces to control the whole of Mesopotamia. Sasanian rule came to its end in 642, with the Arabs' victory at Nihavend, near Kermanshah. Yazdegird was forced to flee northeast. In 651, he was murdered in the region of modern Turkmenistan.

A lasting monument of Sasanian rule in Mesopotamia is the main liwan of the royal palace in Ctesiphon, built by Chosroes I in the sixth century CE.

Without any doubt, the end of the Sasanian rule marked a decisive break in the history of Mesopotamia. Yet in acknowledging the importance of this event in world history, we should not overlook the continuity expressed in the unaltered settlement behavior in Babylonia and the unbroken prosperity of the land.

11 The Islamic Conquest (622–1258)

The year 622 brought a fundamental change to the East. It was in that year that a middle-aged merchant left his hometown Mekka on the Arabian Peninsula, traveled west to the city of Yathrib, a journey that took several days, and settled there. The merchant was, of course, Muhammad. The date of his arrival at the city (later renamed Medina) became known as the Hijrah and was taken as the basis of the Muslim calendar. For about ten years, Muhammad had been having visions, which continued until his death in the year 632, in which an angel had revealed to him the words of God. The record of these visions became the Quran.

Muhammad saw himself first as a prophet sent to the Arab people; later, after the Hijrah, he strengthened his mission, giving it a universal scope. The religion to which Muhammad gave the name of Islam may be characterized as radical monotheism: Muslims believe that there is only one God (Allah) and that Muhammad was his last prophet. As set forth in the Quran, God established certain laws and ritual practices; obedience to these will be rewarded with eternal life in Paradise; disobedience, punished in hell. Among the religious duties of Muslims are ritual prayers five times a day, fasting during the holy month of Ramadan, giving alms, and a pilgrimage to holy places in Mekka and its surroundings. During the last ten years of his life, by his teachings and by means of jihad (holy war), Muhammad put an end to the polytheism and animism of the Arab Peninsula. In Medina he became also a successful politician and overcame many obstacles in order to transform his young religious community into a prosperous state. Muhammad's claim of religious and political influence, however, reached much farther than the Arab Peninsula. Convinced that God had commanded him to bring his message to all mankind, he required the rulers of the neighbouring great empires north and east of Arabia to follow him and to adhere to his teachings. During his own lifetime and even more under the caliphs, his successors, the Muslim state quickly expanded. While it was not among the strategic goals of the Muslim leaders that the indigenous population should accept Islam, they did insist that Islamic law be followed and that political power be in Muslim hands.

From the beginning, Islam recognized Judaism, Christianity, and Zoroastrianism as revealed religions. But although Islam accepts the scriptures of "the people of the book" (Jews, Christians, and Zoroastrians) as the word of God, it considers those scriptures as having been manipulated, which explains their difference from the Quran. Only by the Quran, Muslims believe, was God properly revealed. In the Muslim state, the people of the book had religious freedom but had to pay a special tax (*jizya*) and were allowed to fulfill military duties only in exceptional cases. Besides the jizya, the new Muslim authorities imposed taxes on land to be paid by Jews, Christians, and Zoroastrians. Later, this land tax was levied regardless of the religious affiliation of the owner.

Politically, a liberal attitude toward non-Muslims made good sense. Vast regions conquered by the Muslim armies were inhabited by a large majority of Christians and others, who could hardly be controlled by the small minority of Muslim overlords. One reason for the Muslims' military and political success was the fact that the Byzantine Empire, which ruled over Mesopotamia, Syria, Palestine, Egypt, and North Africa, regarded some of its Christian subjects as heretics and tried to convert them, often by force, to its own orthodoxy. Under Muslim rule, the various Christian confessions in the East could develop free of any religio-political influence. So it is not surprising that many Christian leaders were willing, or even eager, to open the gates of their cities to Muslim armies and thus get rid of the hated Byzantine rule.

Mesopotamia was one of the first regions outside of the Arab Peninsula to be invaded by Muslim armies. Parts of the lower Euphrates came under Muslim domination more or less by chance. Under the rule of the first caliph, Abu Bakr (632–634), a military force was sent to Bahrain to suppress an insurrection. After accomplishing their mission, the soldiers turned northward without Abu Bakr's knowledge and gained control over the Shatt al-Arab delta region. In the spring of 636, the Arab military leader Sa'd ibn Abi Waqqas gained a decisive victory at Qadisiya over the Persian ruler, Yazdegird, and acquired ample booty when he seized the Persian capital, Ctesiphon (near today's Baghdad). From several strongholds in Mesopotamia, Muslim armies continued to make conquests in Iran and Syria. These strongholds, cities that had developed from military camps and were thus inhabited only by Muslims, served as both political and military centers of Muslim rule. The two major cities were Basra, a port, and Kufa, which had been developed as a center of power by Ali ibn Abi Talib, the fourth caliph. The rapid expansion of the Islamic state, with structures that were new to Muslims, gave rise to centrifugal forces within the Muslim community. Conflicts developed between the peripheral strongholds and the central authority on the Arabian Peninsula, yet even these tensions did little to reduce the tempo of Islamic expansion.

The most serious internal conflict resulted in two Islamic sects, the Sunni and the Shia, whose differences had begun soon after Muhammad's death. When Muhammad died after a short illness, no rules of succession existed. Ali, the Prophet's cousin and son-in-law, claimed the position of head of the community because of his close kinship to Muhammad. When Abu Bakr was chosen as caliph, Ali reluctantly accepted the choice. But a group of his followers, who became known as *shi'at Ali* (the party of Ali), remained loyal to him. When Ali came to power in 656, he had to fight a number of oppositional groups, especially in the southern part of Mesopotamia.

In 661, Ali was killed. The Muslim governor of Damascus, Mu'awiya, seized power and founded the first Islamic dynasty, that of the Umayyads. Numerous revolts against his rule and that of his successors were started by Muslims in Mesopotamia. So the Umayyad rulers thought it necessary to appoint ruthless men as governors for this province, but that policy merely resulted only in even greater hatred of the dynasty and its representatives. An uprising with lasting consequences took place in 680 in the city of

FIGURE 75. Shiite prayer stones

Kufa. The leaders of the revolt asked Hussein, the son of Ali and grandson of Muhammad, to come from Medina and lead their movement, lending it the prestige of his genealogy. When Hussein's small caravan was approaching Kufa, the revolt had already collapsed. On the plains of Kerbela, Hussein and his group were attacked by superior Umayyad forces, and none survived. From a military point of view, it was nothing but a skirmish, but the consequences for the religious and political development of Islam were vast. The followers of Hussein glorified his death and endowed it with religious significance. They were, and still are, sure that Hussein knew in advance that his journey would prove fatal but willingly chose martyrdom to atone for the sins of mankind. At the same time, the doctrine of Ali's and Hussein's followers, now known as the Shia, taught that all political power outside the family of the Prophet and his kin is illegitimate. This idea is still accepted by a majority of today's Shia.

A perhaps even more important Shia dogma was that every true Muslim needs the guidance of the Prophet and of his kinsmen, the imams, to achieve eternal salvation. The chain of imams varies. Most Shia believed that there were twelve imams. They were also convinced that the last imam was living in secret and would return one day as Mahdi (messiah). When Mahdi appears, he will found an empire of justice and peace that will last a thousand years. And only after that period will the Day of Judgment come. This millenarian conviction is held by all Shiites still today. Since most of the twelve imams have their tombs in Mesopotamia, and since visiting their graves is rewarded by God, Shiite communities developed around imam tombs in Kerbela, Najaf, Kazimiya, and Samarra, influencing the history of the Shiites to this day, both inside and outside Iraq.

From the point of view of the Umayyad rulers in Damascus, but also from that of modern observers, Mesopotamia lay on the geographic borderland between the Arab and the Iranian worlds. Initially, Islam was an Arab religion. But with the political expansion of the Muslim rule came an ethnic expansion of the new religion. Arabs asked for a special status within the Muslim community. That status was resented by new, non-Arab Muslims in Iran or Central Asia, which led to uprisings, especially in Iran and Mesopotamia, in the form of millenarian movements with strong nativistic elements, expressed in Shiite or proto-Shiite language. Central to conflicts was the question of who held the right to rule over Muslims. The instigators of the revolts preached that this right belonged to the family of the Prophet Muhammad, the *ahl al-bait*. The Umayyads generally managed to suppress this kind of opposition, but when the dynasty itself became greatly weakened by internal strife, it fell victim to the Abbasid revolution.

The Abbasid movement began by stressing the right of the *ahl al-bait* to power, but then expanded that right to the descendants of Abbas, a half-brother of the Prophet's father. The leader of the movement was Abu Muslim, a gifted agitator and strategist. He took advantage of the discontent of new Iranian Muslims and even gained the support of Zoroastrian and Buddhist princes against the Umayyads. His propaganda was millenarian in character. To symbolize the movement, he chose black flags, which at the time were believed to signify the imminent coming of the Mahdi. By 746, he had won political and religious control over most of Iran. Four years later, Abbasid troops chased the Umayyads out of Iraq.

The Name "Iraq" is derived from two Arabic geographical designations: al-'Iraq al-'arabi (the Arabic Iraq) for the delta region of the Tigris and the Euphrates, and al-'Iraq al-'ajami (the Persian Iraq) for the mountainous regions east and northeast of the river valley. The leader of the Abbasid movement, Abu l-Abbas, was proclaimed caliph and took the official name al-Saffah. This name,

FIGURE 76. Tomb of Zubayda, wife of Harun al-Rashid; one of the oldest buildings in Baghdad

meaning "the one who donates generously," is significant for the millenarian aspects of the Abbasid movement, since generosity is one of the attributes of the Mahdi.

In the first chapter of its history, the new dynasty achieved political and military consolidation. One action seen as necessary was the killing of the charismatic Abu Muslim, who was understood as a danger to the power of the Abbasid family. The Shiites were disappointed in their hopes, because the Abbasids made clear that they would stick to Sunni orthodoxy. The final consolidation of power was the work of the second caliph, al-Mansur (754–775), who founded the city of Baghdad in 762. Under him and his successors, including Harun ar-Rasheed (786–809), the new city on the river Tigris became one of the most splendid and fascinating capitals in the world. Baghdad attracted legions of artists and scientists. Under the rule of al-Ma'mun (813–833), philosophical, medical, and technical texts were translated in great numbers from Greek into Arabic, often via Aramaic, and published in lavishly ornamented manuscripts (fig. 77). Visitors marveled at huge mosques with well-stocked libraries, at magnificent palaces with extensive gardens. In the markets and in bazaars of Baghdad, products from all four corners of the world were offered. The population of the city consisted of Muslims from all regions of the Abbasid Empire, as well as large communities of Jews, Christians, and Zoroastri-

FIGURE 77. Illustration from
an Arabic translation of a
Greek medical manuscript

ans. Diplomats from countries around the world paid visits to the
caliph's court.

Al-Mansur established a system of central government, administered from Baghdad with the vizier as chief. For several decades,
members of the Barmakide family, originally from Iran, held this
position. By their participation in political decision-making, Iranian influence on the new dynasty and its capital was strengthened.
For example, Sasanian administrative techniques and elements of
court etiquette were introduced. At the same time, Iranian literary
and cultural traditions crept in, as indicated by the introduction
of Iranian literary forms and themes or the influence of Iranian
culinary traditions on the cuisine of the Abbasid elite. In architecture too, Sasanian elements were found, such as the famous liwan.
This Iranian influence, however, came at the cost of Arab tribal
solidarity. In place of that solidarity, Sunni orthodoxy was stressed,
becoming a common ideological basis of the cosmopolitan Abbasid
Empire. Meanwhile, with his strengthening religious position, the
caliph acquired more authority than the Sunni doctors. The caliph
al-Ma'mud (d. 833), for example, introduced the Mu'tazila, the
only Sunni sect that was a rationalistic form of Islam, inspired by

FIGURE 78. Ruins of the Friday Mosque of al-Mutawakkil at Samarra

Hellenistic philosophy. But the sect died out for several reasons, one of the more important being the great extension of the empire.

Only fifty years later, the empire proved too vast to be controlled permanently by the administrative, communicative, and technical means of that time. In regions far from Baghdad, dynasties established themselves and acted independently of the caliphal authority. The need for the caliph's formal consent to the investiture of any regional ruler remained the caliph's sole means of demonstrating his overlordship. When taxes from these regions were no longer sent to Baghdad, the caliph's only way or raising money for the maintenance of his court was to sell his consent to investitures. In some parts of the empire, local dynasties like the Fatimid dynasty in Egypt refused to accept the overlordship of the Abbasid caliph for religious reasons. Lengthy military conflicts resulted, which further weakened the authority of the caliph. Even in Iraq, the caliphs lost more and more of their power, in part because of the fragmentation of the Muslim religion. Some of the religious groups tried to convert other Muslims by force of arms. In periods of weak central power, groups like these could hold out in the marshy regions of southern Iraq for decades, creating insecurity for travelers, traders, and even the central administrative authorities.

Many of the caliphs were manipulated by their personal guards, who were mostly of Turkish origin. Internal strife broke out from

FIGURE 79. Wall
painting in al-
Mutawakkil's palace
in Samarra

time to time between these guards and the population of Baghdad,
prompting the caliph al-Mu'tasim (833–842) to establish a new
capital north of Baghdad, called Samarra. But the caliphs who
lived there were even more grossly subjected to the will of their
Praetorian guards. The caliph al-Mutawakkil therefore returned
to Baghdad to enlist the help of citizens and the Muslim scholars
to break the guards' power. Success was not granted to him. In
945, he fell under the total control of the Shiite dynasty of the
Buyides, who determined the politics of heartland of the Abbasid
Empire for many years. The caliphate became a titular institution,
representing only Sunni Islam.

In the twelfth and thirteenth centuries, Iraq found itself in a
difficult strategic position between the armies of the Mamluk sultanate in Egypt and Syria to the west, and the Mongolian armies
pushing in from the east. Some of the caliphs, primarily the wily
al-Nasir (1180–1225), tried to turn this situation to the advantage
of the caliphate. Al-Nasir asked the Mongolian commanders for
help against a rebellion in Iran. The Mongols had expanded from
Central Asia into regions south of the Black Sea and the Caspian
Sea. But soon it became clear that the Mongolians presented a
lethal danger to the Abbasid caliphate. In 1258, Mongolian forces

under the command of Hulagu, grandson of Ghengis Khan, seized Baghdad. Arab historians inform us that the conquerors erected pyramids of human skulls. The most magnificent city in the Near East was looted and destroyed. This catastrophe also marked the end of the Abbasid caliphate. An Abbasid quasi caliphate survived in Cairo under Mamluk control until 1517, when the Ottoman sultan Mehmet Fatih took over the title of caliph.

Iraq was ruled for a while by the Mongols. Eventually the Mongols accepted Islam and were influenced by Muslim cultural traditions, but there was no assimilation; the Iraqi land and people remained alien to them. Following internal clashes among various branches of the Mongolian ruling clans, Baghdad was conquered a second time in 1339. This time it was Timur (also known as Tamerlane) who managed to control the Mongolian empire, but only for a short time. Arab historians tell us that the Mongols also destroyed Mesopotamia's complex irrigation system, which had undergirded the prosperity of the country. But blame for the disaster, whose consequences are felt even today, should also be laid upon the Mongols' adversaries in battle, the Mamluk troops. Both sides tried to gain a superior military position by a scorched-earth policy and, in so doing, they destroyed the economic and material basis of the population of Iraq and northern Syria. With the irrigation system destroyed, the region became depopulated. As a result of depopulation, knowledge concerning the creation and upkeep of artificial irrigation and the equitable distribution of water—knowledge that had been passed on by word of mouth—was lost. In an astonishingly short period, most parts of Iraq turned into desert. A large proportion of the remaining population, which had been sedentary, assumed a nomadic life. Baghdad was reduced to a small provincial town, and other cities in Iraq to mere villages, often controlled by nomadic tribes. It was not until the second half of the twentieth century that Iraq recovered from the catastrophe of 1258.

12 Iraq as Part of the Ottoman Empire
(1258–1918)

The three hundred years following the destruction of Baghdad can be divided into four periods. For the first eighty years, the region was ruled from Iran by the Mongolian Ilkhanids. For another eighty years, Baghdad was the capital of a Mongolian fiefdom ruled by the Jal'irid dynasty. The region was then taken over for 120 years by the Turkoman tribal dynasties of the Karakoyunlu and the Akoyunlu. And in 1508, it became part of the growing Safavid kingdom of Iran. In the autumn of 1533, however, the Safavid governor had to leave Baghdad, lacking the power to defend the city against the attacks of an Ottoman army under the command of the sultan Suleyman I, known as Suleyman the Magnificent.

After centuries of a weak political and administrative leadership, Iraq became part of a strong, well-organized empire. Since the Ottomans were especially interested in the city of Baghdad and its surrounding land, Baghdad became one of the main administrative centers in Iraq. Basra, in the south, also grew in importance for the Ottomans; its harbor was strategically vital for the developing confrontations with the fleets of expanding European powers, including Portugal, Spain, and England. Basra was the door for all economic activities, especially trade, in Iraq and even in Syria and Egypt. We hear of Mosul, another major administrative center for the Ottomans, only fifty years after the Ottoman conquest, probably because the northern part of Iraq was earlier governed from the city of Aleppo in northern Syria. The first names of pashas heading the administration of northern Iraq from Mosul can be found in sources from the beginning of the seventeenth century.

We do not know how powerful the Ottoman administration

FIGURE 80. Miniature painting of the type of ship used in the Persian Gulf

really was. The Ottoman pashas may not have extended their influence beyond the city walls, at least in Basra and Baghdad. The countryside was controlled by the leaders of various tribal confederations, who controlled the caravan routes between the central cities and dominated even the provincial towns. The Ottomans had to bribe the tribes with money and privileges in order to secure their loyalty. Tribal control of the small towns had social as well as political consequences. Town dwellers adopted the ethical norms and social structures of the nomads. In the administrative capitals, however, the Ottoman administrators did establish a certain degree of law and order. One problem for Iraq was its situation between the Ottoman and the Iranian empires, which had been archenemies for centuries. It thus furnished a battleground for Ottoman and Iranian troops, and portions of Iraqi territory changed from one side to the other and back again. Another problem was that the pashas in charge of the administration in Basra, Baghdad, and Mosul were transferred to other places after short periods of service, so they never had time to get to know their administrative region well and often had no interest in its problems.

Taking advantage of the constant change in governors, a Janissary officer called Bakr unofficially seized power in Baghdad. Bakr held the rank of *su-bashi,* a person overseeing water supplies but later also the title of police commander in the Ottoman ranking system. When his enemies tried to do away with him, he declared himself officially the ruler, a serious affront to the Ottoman sultan in Istanbul. Troops were sent to Baghdad to remove the usurper from his position, but various military encounters had no definitive result. Bakr then asked the shah of Iran to come for help. Shah Abbas (1587–1629) took the opportunity to bring Iraq under his control, in part because most of the Shiite holy places were located there, and Shia was the official religion of Iran. He forced back the Ottoman troops, and on November 28, 1623, he entered Baghdad. The Sunni families in Baghdad had to bear the heaviest burden of the Iranian occupation. It was thanks to the intervention of Shiite religious leaders that at least some of the Sunni inhabitants of Baghdad could survive the ordeal. Of course, the Ottoman side tried to regain the lost positions in Iraq. Sultan Murad IV (1623–1640) regained control over Baghdad on December 25, 1688. Now it was the Shiite population that had to bear the hardships of occupation. The Ottomans failed to learn from this experience. The short terms of office for governors returned, and the pashas paid little attention to the needs and problems of the people. But in 1649 another new governor, the pasha Ahmed, came to Baghdad and stayed there for a whole year, trying to improve the situation; a grateful population called him the "angel governor." He acknowledged administrative errors, particularly in the field of taxation. When he returned to Istanbul and became grand vizier, he introduced reforms to correct those errors. To improve tax revenue for the empire, Ahmed auctioned tax-levying licenses to bidders in the various regions of the empire. In this way he secured the revenue but made things harder for the population. The tax collectors were not interested in improving the economy but were eager to be compensated for their expenses and to keep for themselves an ample portion of the money they collected for the empire.

Mosul, being closer geographically than Basra to the Ottoman center of power in Istanbul, enjoyed a more stable existence. Basra's situation improved for other reasons. Since the beginning of the seventeenth century, a man of Turkoman origin named Afrasiyab had held power in that port city and the area around it. He managed to secure his position by collaborating with the Portuguese fleet that operated in the Persian Gulf, so that he could defend himself against Iranian attacks. Afrasiyab, as well as his son and successor, acknowledged the supremacy of the Ottoman sultan but did not follow his orders or pay taxes to him.

When the pasha Hasan became governor in Baghdad in 1704, Iraq took a different turn politically, a situation that lasted 130 years. Hasan was able to govern independently of Istanbul and was the first of a series of rulers whom Iraqi historians called the Mamluk Dynasty. He was followed by his son Ahmed. Subsequently, a series of Mamluks originating from the Caucasus took power in Mesopotamia. They acknowledged the sovereignty of the Ottoman sultan and sent gifts and declarations of loyalty to the Sublime Porte, but they governed more or less independently. It was during Hasan's and Ahmed's administration that Baghdad gained preeminence over Basra and Mosul. For a time, a representative of the pasha of Baghdad ruled in Basra. In Mosul, the Jailili family ruled for a time, maintaining independence from Istanbul. Between 1722 and 1747, however, Iraq was once again a theater of war between the old enemies Iran and the Ottoman Empire. The empire usually prevailed, often by luck.

Since the late eighteenth century, a new danger, besides Iran, had been emerging for Iraq. To its south, on the Arabian Peninsula, a radical Muslim sect called the Wahhabi established itself. The sect was founded by the Muslim scholar Ibn Abd al-Wahhab (1703–1793) and the leader of the Bedouin tribe, the Saud. They had fundamentalist ideas and abhorred all deviations from their idea of Islam. They pursued Shiites with particular venom. Again and again, Wahhabi troops invaded the southern part of Iraq, attacking, among other places, the holy cities of Kerbela and Najaf in 1811. In reaction to these attacks, leading Shiite scholars intensified their efforts to convert the neighboring Bedouin groups to Shia. At the same time they set up their own militias to defend the holy cities.

Another political actor appeared in Iraq during this period: the East India Company. Since the end of the eighteenth century, representatives of that British company had been crossing Mesopotamia regularly on their way to India. The company had established a regular postal service by camel between Aleppo in Syria and Baghdad. Company agents had secured the good graces of the Baghdad pashas by providing modern weapons and sending military instructors. In 1802, a British consulate opened its doors in Baghdad. The more powerful the East India Company became, and with it the British consuls in Baghdad, the more strained the relations between the British and the Mamluks. Both the number and the intensity of conflicts between the parties increased, which led to a rapid decline of the Mamluks' power. In Egypt, in the meantime, the Khedivial dynasty had made itself virtually independent of the Sublime Porte, so the sultan could no longer tolerate any autonomy in Iraq. Again luck was on the Ottoman side. In 1830, a serious epidemic that had spread from Iran killed many of the Mamluks' soldiers and their Bedouin auxiliaries, allowing Ottoman troops quite easily to gain direct control over Iraq again after more that a century.

The reestablishment of Ottoman power in Iraq was followed by a number of administrative reforms. The province of Mosul was put under Baghdad's control, while Basra was administered directly from Istanbul. All the reforms that had taken place in the central areas of the Ottoman Empire since the beginning of the nineteenth century—first under the sultanate of Mahmud II (1808–1839), and reaching a peak under the sultanate of Abd al-Majid (1839–1861) with the Gülhane's Khatt-i Sharif decree—were enacted in Iraq also. The Ottoman reform movements of the so-called Tanzimat period were strengthened by the Khatt-i Humayun decree of 1856. In practice, however, the ideas of the Ottoman reformers were not very successful, especially in the provinces, including Iraq. The rapidly changing appointments that had been one of the mistakes of the former Ottoman administration continued, and none of the governors had time to implement the reforms. Some governors saw the Baghdad post as a dip in their career, others even as a penalty. If they were not moved to another post quickly, they did everything they could to be transferred, especially to Istanbul. In consequence, a special class of administrative specialists developed in Baghdad, known as effendis. They all came from Baghdad families and all had a Sunni Arab background, but they had become very Turkish in orientation. Normally the children of these effendis were sent to Istanbul at an early age to receive training in Ottoman administration or in the military. There they rose in the Ottoman hierarchies, often marrying women of the Ottoman-Turkish upper class. Many returned to Baghdad feeling profoundly distant to their homeland. The effendis tried to make no mistakes that might endanger their own career. Because they were afraid that negative results would pose too high a personal risk to themselves, they were not interested in implementing the reforms. So political, economic, and cultural life in Iraq barely changed. The police who were supposed to protect the public in the big cities were poorly paid and did a poor job. Equally bad was public administration. In the countryside, sheikhs of Bedouin tribes determined political and economic development. In the Shiite centers, the leading religious scholars with their personal militias and bodyguards forced their religious and social norms upon the rest of the population.

One of the most important Ottoman reformers, Midhat Pasha, was governor of Baghdad from 1869 to 1872. In this very backward province of the Ottoman Empire, he tried to introduce a few reforms, including improvement of the river system and granting the local population some input into governmental decisions that concerned them. For that he established city and village councils. He had many public buildings erected. He founded a newspaper, an arms factory, hospitals, orphanages, and a tramway between Baghdad and its northern Shiite suburb Kazimiya. His period of service in Baghdad was short, however, and few of his reforms were successfully implemented. Later, he served several terms as grand vizier in Istanbul but had no opportunity to improve the situation in Iraq. Because of his conflicts with the autocratic sultan Abd al-Hamid II (1876–1908), he was stripped of political power and eventually, in 1883, was murdered.

Political and social development in Iraq, of course, was closely related not only to the situation in Istanbul but also to what was going on in the rest of the world. Since the mid-nineteenth century, the Ottoman Empire had degenerated to the point of being called "the sick man at the Bosporus." The major powers of that time did not conceal their interest in inheriting the invalid's estate. There was considerable competition among Germany, Russia, France, and Britain to secure their share of the booty and to gain control over the eastern Mediterranean as well. The British, traditionally in a strong position, tried to enhance their influence by signing treaties with Bedouin sheikhs and emirs, promising them aid and cooperation, although such agreements were totally unjustified from the point of international law. The strategic goal was to safeguard the sea route to India, a crown colony of the British Empire. A century later, in 1991, one of these treaties, with the emir of Kuwait, was used to justify the first allied invasion of Iraq. Germany tried to gain more economic influence not only in the heartland of the Ottoman Empire but also in its Mesopotamian province. The best-known manifestation of this policy was the construction of the famous Baghdad railway, begun in 1899 with German financial and technical support. The German position was strengthened when the Committee for Union and Progress, a group of young Ottoman officers later called the Young Turks, succeeded in deposing the sultan Abd al-Hamid II in 1908. The driving force in the committee was Enver Pasha, a young officer who had received his general staff training in Germany and had served several years as military attaché in Berlin. Strategic considerations such as the ongoing confrontation with Russia, combined with a strong personal relationship, led the Ottoman Empire in 1915 to take the German side in the First World War. In the same year, a British expeditionary force landed near Basra but was heavily defeated near the cities of Kut and Amara in southern Iraq. It was not until 1918 that the British gained control over Mosul and hence over the whole of Iraq. The defeat of the Central Powers spelled the end of the Ottoman Empire and a new period for Mesopotamia.

13 Iraq under the Monarchy (1921–1958)

While the First World War was still under way, Britain and France were debating the future of the Middle East. In the famous Sykes-Picot agreement, which was kept secret during the war, the two allies decided that the three Ottoman provinces of Basra, Baghdad, and Mosul should come under British control. That was the diplomatic basis of the military control of these regions exercised by the British from 1918 onward, a situation that was not accepted by the local population and met with heavy resistance. Representatives of the Iraqi population argued that they too were entitled to self-determination, a right proclaimed by U.S. President Wilson at the end of the war. Quite soon, the call for an independent Iraq, from Basra in the south to Mosul in the north, could be heard in Baghdad and in the Shiite centers of Kerbela and Najaf. In the north, some politicians were demanding an independent Kurdish state, but there were no clear ideas about the boundaries either of that state or of an independent Iraq. The British military administration, which was under the command of the India Office in London, ignored the Kurdish demands and established an administrative structure for the whole country. Even in the smallest provincial towns, British officers were in charge. Most of these officers were young and had no experience in dealing with an Arab population. In 1919, tension between British administrative personal and the Iraqi population rose continuously. In the spring of 1920, a popular uprising erupted all over Iraq; Iraqi historians later called it the Revolution of 1920.

These uprisings may be said to have triggered the development of an Iraqi national identity. A coalition was formed—Sunnis and Shiites; Muslims, Jews, and Christians; Arabs, Kurds, and Turkomans—all of them opposed to the British rule. Shiite scholars preached in Sunni mosques, and Shiite preachers took part in the Sunni celebration of the Prophet's birthday. Christian and Jewish clergy visited the Shiite shrines of Kazimiya in a northern suburb of Baghdad. Although the coalition achieved some military success, the uprising was eventually subdued by the British, who used air attacks for the first time in the Middle East. Ultimately, however, the costs of enforcing British rule in Iraq were so high that the British Parliament demanded a political solution.

After lengthy discussions, the "Kingdom of Iraq" was founded under the mandate of the League of Nations. Great Britain, as a member of the League, continued to control political development in Iraq. Emir Faysal, from the Hashemite family of the sharifs of Mecca, was installed as king of Iraq in 1921. During the First World War, Faysal had fought beside the British against the Ottoman army. The British had promised him a great Arab kingdom that would be independent of them, but they did not keep their word. At first, the Iraqi population accepted the king, though they would have preferred his brother Abdallah, who became king of the neighboring Trans-Jordan. Faysal could prove that he was from the family of the Prophet Muhammad, so when he marched north from Basra to Baghdad and visited the Shiite shrines at Kerbela and Najaf on the way, Iraqi newspapers headlined: "Faysal at the tombs of his grandfathers." Especially the Shiite majority in Iraq made it very clear to the king that they would not tolerate close cooperation with the British. But Faysal could not avoid such cooperation, given the strength of the British and his own lack of any reliable power structure. Every Iraqi functionary of Faysal's administration had a British adviser at his side, who always prevailed in the event of disagreement.

When Iraq became a full member of the League of Nations in 1932 and thus gained formal independence, the British continued to exert their influence. The Shiite population grew even more restless, but the British and the new Iraqi government reacted swiftly and expelled the leading Shiite agitators. One of the Shiites' major grievances was that all important positions in administration and politics were held by former Ottoman officers of Sunni origin, and most of these had never before lived in Iraq. All of them had arrived with Faysal. The most important of these political figures was Nuri al-Said, who served a number of times as foreign minister or defense minister before becoming prime minister and who always sided with the British. With the Shiite agitation quelled, the Sunnis improved their own position. The Shiites reacted by boycotting a referendum concerning the Iraqi constitution, and even refused to participate in governing the country. When they understood the consequences of their denial, the major positions in government, army, and administration were already in Sunni hands. All that remained for the Shiites were posts in the ministry of education or similar institutions, which carried no weight in political decision-making. From that time on, the Shiite majority saw themselves treated like a minority in their own country. As the heroes of the "Revolution of 1920," they were particularly embittered because of their exclusion from governing the country whose independence they had won.

Politics in Iraq between the two world wars was marked by two tendencies. On the one hand, tensions rose between the various religious and ethnic groups. Shiites and Kurds opposed the Sunni-Arab dominance in the country, a situation they blamed on the British. On the other hand, a very strong Arab nationalism developed in Iraq, which was especially attractive to young people. Opposition to the British influence in Iraq naturally gained strength. At the same time, Fascism was on the rise in Europe, and Fascists seized power in Germany and Italy. Many Iraqis sympathized with the ideology. Young Iraqis traveled to Germany to study. In Iraq, a national youth organization was founded on the model of the Hitler-Jugend. Iraqi Arab nationalists were outraged by the British toleration of Jewish immigration to Palestine. In 1939, the Iraqi nationalist government under Rashid Ali al-Gailani rejected the British request that Iraq join Britain in declaring war on Germany, and insisted on remaining neutral. In 1941, when British troops planned to cross Iraq from the south on their way to Palestine, the Iraqi government considered it a violation of the country's neutrality, declared war on Britain, and attacked the British troops. After a short battle, the Iraqis were defeated. The German assistance they had counted on never materialized. Rashid Ali al-Gailani and other nationalistic politicians went into exile in Germany, where they stayed until the end of the war. In Iraq, a pro-British government was installed, which suppressed all opposition by invoking martial law.

After World War II and with the beginning of the cold war, Iraq was entailed in the Western strategy of containment of the Warsaw-pact countries. With Turkey, which was and still is a member of NATO, and with Iran and Pakistan, Iraq became a member of the Baghdad Treaty. But since the beginning of the 1950s, politics in the Middle East had influenced Iraq also. The success of Nasser's "Free Officers" in the anticolonial struggle in Egypt, along with Nasser's ascent to the status of hero to the Arab masses, weakened the position of Nuri al-Said's pro-British government. That position was further undermined by the barely noticed but effective activity of the Baath Party, founded in Syria in the 1940s. Nuri al-Said attempted to counteract the strong pan-Arabic tide by unifying the two Hashemite kingdoms of Iraq and Jordan. In the meantime, the Communist Party in Iraq was gaining adherents among the new class of workers in the oil industry and among the impoverished peasant population that had fled from the oppression of rural landlords and settled in the cities. Their life remained equally wretched in the slums of Baghdad, Basra, and Mosul. The second half of the 1950s saw continual antigovernment demonstrations and other forms of popular protest by various oppositional groups and organizations. In the north, a small-scale war for independence was being waged by Kurdish militias under the legendary leader Mullah Mustafa Barazani against the central government in Baghdad. Most of the Iraqi elite had grown indifferent to the realities of the political and economic life of the country. Nuri el-Said told a European journalist that the bullet that would kill him had not yet been cast. In early morning of July 14, 1958, a tank brigade under the command of General Abd al-Karim Qassem attacked the royal palace, occupied the main radio station, and attempted to take Nuri al-Said prisoner. The prime minister escaped from his house, but while trying to reach the American Embassy he was trapped in the streets and lynched by the crowd. The young king Faysal II and most of the royal family were killed. It was announced on Iraqi Radio that the monarchy had come to an end and a "Revolutionary Command Council" (RCC) had taken over.

14 The Republic of Iraq (1958–2008)

Between the revolution of 1958 and the year 1968, when the Arab Socialist Baath Party came to power, Iraq experienced nonstop political insecurity and ideological antagonism. For the first few months of General Qassem's regime, there was a feeling of openness and optimism in all strata of Iraqi society. The rigid formalization that had characterized the final years of the monarchy seemed to be over, and a new age appeared to have dawned. But ideological differences and personal tensions soon made themselves felt within the Revolutionary Command Council. The two leaders of the revolution, General Qassem and his former aide-de-camp, Colonel Abd al-Salam Aref, had different ambitions. Qassem was charismatic and ideologically independent; Aref, on the other hand, was deeply impressed by the Egyptian leader Gamal Abd al-Nasser and his ideology of pan-Arab Nasserism. Both had almost no experience in practical politics. Aref wanted Iraq to join the United Arab Republic, which had come into being shortly before the Iraqi revolution by the union of Egypt and Syria and, later, Yemen. Qassem strongly opposed this scheme. Aref, by then minister of the interior, tried several times to replace Qassem, who reacted by removing Aref from his ministry and sending him as military attaché to West Germany. The tensions between the two men had consequences at all levels of the officer corps and led to a general politicization of the military forces. Nasserites and Arab-Iraqi nationalists were soon at loggerheads. Yet the two factions stood together in their opposition to the Iraqi Communist Party, which had founded its own militia and exerted a powerful influence on organizations such as trade unions and women's or

FIGURE 81. General Abd
al-Karim Qassem

teachers' associations. During the five years of his rule, General
Qassem's policies shifted between support of the Nasserites, the
Iraqi Nationalists, and the Communists.

In March 1959, officers influenced by Nasser's ideas attempted
a putsch against Qassem, which was suppressed with the help of
the Communists. In July of the following year, the Turkoman
population in the oil city of Kirkuk was subjected to massacres,
said to have been organized by Communists. After a brief interlude
of peace, Kurdish nationalists rose again in northern Iraq. On October 7, 1959, a group of Baathists, among them Saddam Hussein,
attempted to assassinate Qassem. After that, Qassem, who was
not seriously wounded, thought himself untouchable and showed
signs of megalomania. He was strongly backed by the poor and
uneducated masses, whose situation, with the help of Communist
organizations, he had improved in many respects. Among such
improvements were a reform of the health system, an initiative for
the establishment of a social security system, and the construction
of modest housing compounds for Baghdad's majority Shiite slum
dwellers. The compound within Baghdad was first called Madinat
al-thawra (City of the Revolution); under Saddam Hussein it was
called Saddam City, and it has now been renamed al-Sadr City.
Under Qassem's regime, the Shiite majority for the first time felt

they were being treated as equals by the government. Looking beyond his own borders, Qassem made tentative approaches to the Soviet Union, thus arousing the distrust of the United States, but he kept a clear distance because he did not want to strengthen Communist influence at home.

In 1961, to divert attention from domestic problems and to show himself a true Arab nationalist, Qassem laid claim to the sheikhdom of Kuwait, which just had become free of British colonial rule. This action met strong resistance from the international community as well as from the Arab League. Qassem found himself increasingly isolated internationally and also lost the support of the top echelons of Iraqi society. On February 8, 1963, a second assassination attempt against Qassem, this time successful, was conducted by a coalition of Baathists and Nasserites under the leadership of Colonel Abd al-Salam Aref. This action is reputed to have been backed by the CIA. After Qassem was shot, his corpse was shown on Iraqi television for days. A new Revolutionary Command Council took over. An early consequence of Aref's success was the widespread suppression of Communists. It was not long before tensions between Baathists and the followers of Aref were felt within the RCC, but Aref managed to oust the Baathists and take full power into his own hands. The new president had gained both political experience and stature during the five years since the 1958 revolution. With the support of Abd al-Rahman al-Bazzaz, a moderate Arab nationalist, he tried to resolve the conflict with the Kurds. At the same time he sought to improve the country's economy, which had suffered under the chaotic politics of Qassem. In the spring of 1966, Abd al-Salam Aref died in a helicopter crash. He was succeeded by his brother Abd al-Rahman Aref, a colorless general who failed to impress the Iraqi public.

On June 17, 1968, the Baath Party achieved another successful coup with the help of some officers of different ideological inclinations. The Baathists were determined not to lose power as they had done in 1963. They quickly got rid of all non-Baathist officers on the Revolutionary Command Council. Hasan al-Bakr, a general who came from Tikrit, a small city north of Baghdad, was proclaimed the new president of Iraq. The ideology of the Baath Party was expressed in its slogan "unity, liberty, and socialism."

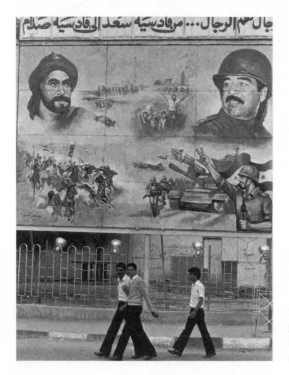

FIGURE 82. Propaganda in Baathist Iraq: Saddam Hussein and Sa'd ibn Abi Waqqas

By "unity," the Baathists were referring to the unity and sanctity of the Arab world, from Morocco to Iraq. By "liberty" they meant political, economic, und cultural independence from any foreign influence. By socialism, they called for the nationalization of all basic industry and major businesses. Small industry and trade could remain in private hands. The leadership of the Iraqi Baath Party, however, was soon riven by infighting, from which Hasan al-Bakr emerged as winner, supported by his nephew Saddam Hussein.

The huge rise in the price of oil in 1973 made Iraq a rich country. The leadership of the Baath Party initiated several programs of social and technological change. The oil industry was successfully nationalized. Large-scale literacy programs were started, and organizations for women, students, workers, and others were established, imbuing the population with Baathist ideology. The regime intensified its policy of secularization, resisting all religious influences on Iraqi society. Some foreign observers described Iraq during this period as a development dictatorship. At the same time, while investing 60 percent of its oil income in military projects, Iraq rose to become a leading regional power.

In June 1979, Saddam Hussein took over the presidency of the Iraqi Republic from his uncle Hasan al-Bakr. The new president was intelligent, unscrupulous, and brutal. While he lacked either military experience or knowledge of international politics, with U.S. support he started a war against Iran, which, then under Ayatollah Khomeini, was thought to be weak after the turmoil of the Islamic Revolution. That proved untrue. The war between Iraq and Iran dragged on from 1980 until 1988, damaging both countries and ending without a victor. Although the Western powers and the Arab oil countries still supported Iraq at the end of the war, the country was weakened politically and economically. After several warnings, and grossly miscalculating the U.S. position, Iraq invaded the neighbouring emirate of Kuwait on August 2, 1990. A coalition under the leadership of the United States drove the Iraqi occupational troops out of Kuwait. Kurds and Shiites responded to an appeal from the U.S. leadership to rise up against Saddam Hussein's dictatorship. But the troops of Saddam Hussein, having been let down by the Americans and their allies, suppressed the uprising mercilessly. In August 1990, the Security Council of the United Nations ordered a strict embargo against Iraq, which had long-lasting economic and social consequences for the country. The Iraqi middle class either left the country or became impoverished. Hundreds of thousands of children died of malnutrition and poor medical care. The leaders of the regime, however, were untouched by the embargo.

After the attack on the World Trade Center on September 11, 2001, the United States government, under President George W. Bush, accused Iraq of cooperating with Islamic terrorists and of still possessing weapons of mass destruction, despite its assurances to the contrary. Neither accusation ever proved correct. After long debates in the United Nations Security Council, the Bush administration decided to invade Iraq without the consent of the international community. Planning this invasion had led to some disagreement between the military and the civil members of the U.S. Department of Defence concerning strategy. In the end, the civilians and the defence secretary, Donald Rumsfeld, gained the upper hand, and a strategy of "shock and awe" was applied. When Turkey withdrew permission for American troops to cross its territory in order to invade Iraq from the north, a coalition of military contingents from Britain, Poland, Spain, and a handful of other nations, all under the command of the U.S. army, invaded from the south, via Kuwait and Saudi Arabia. The invasion began on March 20, 2003; by April 8, the Iraqi army had ceased to resist.

At the beginning of the occupation of Iraq, most of the population took a cautious but not unfriendly attitude toward the foreign troops. But when the occupiers, especially the Americans, appeared unwilling or unable to guarantee public safety in Baghdad and elsewhere, rioting took place for days, without interference from the foreign troops. It soon became obvious that U.S. personnel in Iraq had no idea how to handle the situation. Administrative leaders changed rapidly. Nor was it clear whether the civilian or the military personnel was in charge. After weeks of turmoil, things grew clearer, but not easier, for the coalition troops. One of the first orders of the U.S. administration in Iraq had been to dissolve the Iraqi army and to discharge all Iraqi civilian functionaries who had been members of the Baath Party. As a result, thousands of former soldiers, many of them still armed, were no longer under coalition control. Highly educated professionals, such as engineers who had served as directors of power plants or water-supply systems, were out of a job, and their institutions were without competent managers. Many members of the technical and intellectual elite left Iraq and started working in other Gulf countries or in the West. Those who could not leave their homeland struggled to survive.

In the following years, the situation deteriorated further, especially in those parts of Iraq under American control. For a time at least, the south under British control seemed more secure. The U.S. army and civilian administration, with only a few friends, faced enemies on several fronts. These included former Iraqi soldiers, particularly members of the Republican Guards and other elite troops. Many were Sunni Arabs, who started to forge coalitions with Sunni Arab tribes. Their uprisings posed the greatest danger in the notorious Sunni Triangle between Baghdad in the east, Ramadi in the west, and the cities of Falluja and Samarra in the north. For months, this region could not be pacified. In late 2003, another player became active there and in many other parts of the country—the al-Qaeda network in Iraq, which operated with terrorist attacks and suicide bombings. This network and its allies directed their attacks not only against U.S. forces but also against various Shiite organizations and militias. The Shiites had successfully assumed many important political and economic positions in Iraq. Having submitted to Sunni leadership since the foundation of Iraq in the 1920s, though always the majority of the population, Shiites were now taking what they considered their due. Sunnis, on the other hand, were convinced that they were the right people to run the country. Afraid they would lose both prestige and their livelihood, they strenuously resisted the Shiite newcomers. The Shiite groups, far from cozy with the U.S. administration, demanded full control of all parts of Iraq that were inhabited by a majority of their coreligionists. Their organizations and militias had one important disadvantage, however. Whereas the Iraqi Shia had traditionally comprised many fractions, it was now further split in three major directions. One group was under the strong influence of Iranian Shiite organizations, partly because of the time these Iraqis had spent in Iranian exile; another was clearly anti-Iranian and advocated a leading role for Shiite Arabs; and a third group had spent years in exile in London and other Western countries. Until recently, these Shiite groups had shared no common political agenda. The central issue for Shiites all over the world is that of religious authority. After debates that had begun in the sixteenth century and lasted two or more centuries, Shiite Islam came to the conclusion that every Muslim believer needs a cleric to guide him (or her) on the right way. Without this leadership, no believer could attain salvation. In consequence, a hierarchy of clerics evolved in Shiite Islam. At the top of this hierarchy is the *marja al-taqlid* ("the source to follow his example"), the highest religious, political, ethical, and economic authority. There is no prescribed rule to elect a *marja al-taqlid*. When the last one, the Ayatollah Abu l-Qasim al-Kho'i, died in Najaf in 1993, no one in the entire Shiite world was considered to be his successor. In the meantime, the Shiite cleric Ali al-Sistani (born about 1930), who lives in Najaf, has become the person likely to assume that mantle. In this person, perhaps, the Shiite Muslims of Iraq will find a common symbol of unity.

By 2008, the war in Iraq had cost the lives of some five thousand American soldiers. The number of Iraqis who died as a result of the war and also of malnutrition, poor medical services, and related factors is estimated somewhere between three and six hundred thousand.

One group in Iraq that did take a positive stance toward the United States was the Kurdish population. During the last years under Saddam Hussein and the Baath party, northern Iraq with its largely Kurdish inhabitants had enjoyed considerable autonomy under the shield of the U.S. air force, which had been flying reconnaissance missions north of the 36th parallel since 1991. Although various Kurdish fractions were competing for supremacy, they all thought it wise to support the U.S. administration in Iraq, not only because of their minority situation but also to protect themselves from Turkish troops. If Turkey were to invade the northern part of Iraq to avoid troubles in its own Kurdish areas, the Kurds in Iraq would risk losing what autonomy they had. To reduce that risk, Kurdish politicians understood that they had to come to terms with the Arab majority in Iraq.

American attempts to quell the insurgency in Iraq by force achieved only limited success. These attempts involved, among other measures, arresting Iraqis suspected of inciting violence and incarcerating them in the old Saddam Hussein prison at Abu Ghraib. In May of 2004, American and other journalists reported that prisoners at Abu Ghraib were being grossly mistreated by the U.S. military. Photos and videos of some of these acts were spread through the media. Although a few soldiers who had inflicted the mistreatment were convicted and sentenced by a U.S. court marshal, the standing of the United States, especially with respect to its policies in the Middle East, was deeply harmed.

Recognizing that Iraq could not be controlled without the cooperation of Iraqi political leaders, the U.S. administration urged that national elections be held as soon as possible. These elections took place in 2005 and 2006, and one of the first orders of business—which took a very long time—was to draft a new Iraqi constitution. Central and regional governments came into being, constructed according to political, religious, and ethnic ratios, but they actually wielded little power. The insurgency continued, and security did not improve. Not just insurgents but common criminals threatened public safety. Kidnapping became a kind of an industry in Iraq. And yet another problem arose, whose solution was beyond the scope of the U.S. and allied forces: in Baghdad and elsewhere in Iraq, where people of different religious and ethnic backgrounds had been living side by side, ethnic and religious cleansing now took place. Kurds living in Baghdad as a minority in Arab neighborhoods, Shiites living among Sunnis, and Sunnis living among Shiites were forced to leave their homes. Not all escaped with their lives. By 2008, most Baghdad neighborhoods were either exclusively Sunni or exclusively Shiite, and few Kurds remained in the city. Religious minorities like the old Christian communities in Iraq were under heavy pressure.

In 2008, the United States army changed its tactics against the uprisings of the Sunni groups. General David Petraeus organized various forms of cooperation with the Sunni tribes, who could no longer tolerate the ruthless acts of al-Quaeda groups not only against foreign soldiers and Shiites but also against Sunni Arabs. This cooperative approach has achieved some success, and security is gradually improving. On the other hand, Iranian influence among the Shiites of Iraq is growing, which may lead again to further Shiite-Sunni strife. At the time of this writing, late 2008, Iraq's future is hanging in the balance.

Chronology, 1600 BCE to 1900 CE

BCE	BABYLONIA		
2600	Mesalim	Royal Cemetery of Ur	
	Urnanshe		
	Eanatum		
	Enmetena		
	Urukagina		
2350	Sargon (2334–2279)	Lugalzagesi of Umma	
	Naramsin (2254–2218)		
	Sharkalisharri (2217–2193)	Gudea of Lagash/Utuhengal of Uruk	
	Urnamma (2112–2095)	(2122–2102)	
2100	Shulgi (2094–2047)		
	Shusin (2037–2029)		
2000	Ibbisin (2028–2004) / Ishbierra (2017–1985)		
	Hammurapi (1792–1750)		
1600	Samsuditana (1626–1595)		**HITTITES**
			Murshili I (1620–1595)
			MITTANI
	KASSITES		Saushtatar (ca. 1440)
	Karaindash (ca.1415)		Artatama (ca. 1420)
1400	Kurigalzu I (ca. 1390)		Tushratta (ca.1390)
	Burnaburiash (ca. 1350)		Shattiwaza (ca. 1330)
			ELAM
			Untash-Napirisha
			(1260–1235)
1200			Shutruk-Nahhunte
	Nebukadnezzar I (1126–1105)		(ca. 1175)
900			**URARTU**
			Sarduri I (ca. 840–830)
800			
	Mardukaplaiddina II		
	(721–710)		
700			
	Mushezibmarduk (692–689)	**MEDIA**	**PERSIA**
		Kyaxares	Cyrus I
	Nabopolassar (626–605)	(ca. 625–585)	(ca. 640–600)
600	Nebukadnezzar II (604–562)		
	Nabonid (555–539)	Astyages	
		(585–550)	Cyrus II (559–530)
			Cambyses II (529–522)
500	Nebukadnezzar III (522)		Darius I (521–486)
			Xerxes I (485–465)
			Artaxerxes I (464–424)
400	Alexander (330–323)		Darius III (335–331)
	Philip III Arrhidaeus (323–316)		

EGYPT

Old Kingdom
Cheops (2551–2520)

Dynasty VI
Pepi I (2300–2268)

MIDDLE KINGDOM
(2040–1785)

2nd INTERM.PERIOD
(1630 –1550)

ASSYRIA

NEW KINGDOM
18th Dynasty

Eriba-Adad (1390–1364)
Assuruballit (1365–1328)

Amenophis III (1391–1353)
Akhenaten (1336–1327)

Shalmaneser I (1273–1244)
Tukulti-Ninurta (1243–1207)

Assurrabi II (1010–970)
Assurnasirpal II (883–859)
Shalmaneser III (858–824)
Shamshiadad V (823–811)
Shammuramat (810–806)
Adadnirari III (805–783)
Tiglathpileser III (744–727)
Sargon II (721–705)
Sennacherib (704–681)
Esarhaddon (680–669)
Assurbanipal (668–631)
Sinsharishkun (627–612)

25th Dynasty
Taharka (690–664)
Tantamun (664–656)
26th Dynasty
Necho II (610–595)
Psamtik II (595–589)

BCE

300	**SELEUCIDS**	Antigonos Monophthalmos (–301)
	Seleucus I Nicator (311–281)	
	Antiochus I Soter (281–261)	**URUK**
	Seleucus II (260–226)	Anuuballit Nikarchos
200	Antiochus III (223–187)	Anuuballit Kephalon (ca.202)
		CHARAX
	Antiochus VII Sidetes	Hyspaosines (165–124)
	(139–129)	
100		

CE

100		
200		
		SASANIANS
		Ardashir I (224–241)
		Shapur I (224–272)
		Bahram I (273–276)
300		Shapur II (309–379)
		Hormizd IV (579–590)
600		Chosroes II (590–628)
	622 Hejira of Mohammed	Hormizd V (631–632)
	632 Death of Mohammed	Chosroes III (632–633)
	Khalif Abu Bakr (632–634)	Yazdigird III (633–651)
	Omar I (634–644)	
	UMAYYADS (651–750)	
	Mu'awiya (660–680)	
	ABBASIDS (750–1256)0800	
	Abul Abbas (750–754)	
	al Mansur (754–775)	
800	al Ma'mun (813–833)1200	
	al Mu'tasim (833–842)	
	al Mutawakkil (847–861)	
1200	al Nasir (1180–1225)	
	Mongol Invasion 1256 under Hülagü	
	2. Mongol Invasion 1339 under Tamerlan	
1500	**OSMAN EMPIRE** (1517–1918)	
	Suleyman the Magnificent (1520–1566)	
	Murad IV (1623–40)	
1900	Abd el Hamid II (1876–1908)	

PARTHIA
Mithrisdates I (171–138)
Phraates II (138–128)
Artabanus II (128–124)
Mithridates II (123–88)

Gotarzes II (38–51)
Osroes (109–128)
Vologases II (106–147)
Mithridates IV (128–147)
Vologases III (148–192)
Vologases IV (191–207)
Artabanus V (208–226)

ROME
Trajan (98–117)
Hadrian (117–138)
Antonius Pius (138–161)
Marc Aurel (161–180)
Commodus (180–192)
Septimius Severus (193–211)

Valerian (253–260)

Constantinus (324–357)

Heraklius I (610–641)

Selected Bibliography

MONOGRAPHS

Adams, Robert McC. *Heartland of Cities: Surveys of Ancient Settlement and Land Use on the Central Floodplains of the Euphrates.* Chicago: University of Chicago Press, 1981.

Adams, Robert McC., and Hans J. Nissen. *The Uruk Countryside: The Natural Setting of Urban Societies.* Chicago: University of Chicago Press, 1972.

Bahrani, Zainab. *The Graven Image: Representation in Babylonia and Assyria.* Philadelphia: University of Pennsylvania Press, 2003.

Baram, Uzi, and Lynda Carroll, eds. *A Historical Archaeology of the Ottoman Empire: Breaking New Ground.* New York: Kluwer Academic/Plenum Publishers, 2000.

Bartl, Karin, and Stefan Hauser, eds. *Continuity and Change in Northern Mesopotamia from the Hellenistic to the Early Islamic Period.* Berlin: Dietrich Reimer Verlag, 1996.

Bottéro, Jean, André Finet, Bertrand Lafont, and Georges Roux. *Everyday Life in Ancient Mesopotamia.* Translated by Antonia Nevill. Baltimore: Johns Hopkins University Press, 2001.

Braidwood, Robert J. The Agricultural Revolution. *Scientific American* 203 (1960): 130–48.

Dalley, Stephanie, trans. and ed. *Myths from Mesopotamia: Creation, the Flood, Gilgamesh, and Others.* Oxford: Oxford University Press, 1989.

Hole, Frank, ed. *The Archaeology of Western Iran: Settlement and Society from Prehistory to the Islamic Conquest.* Washington DC: Smithsonian Institution Press, 1987.

Insoll, Timothy. *The Archaeology of Islam.* Oxford: Blackwell, 1999.

Kuhrt, Amélie. *The Ancient Near East, c. 3000–330 B.C..* 2 vols. London: Routledge, 1995.

Moortgat, Anton. *The Art of Ancient Mesopotamia: The Classical Art of the Near East.* Translated by Judith Filson. London: Phaidon, 1969.

Nissen, Hans J. *The Early History of the Ancient Near East, 9000–2000 B.C.* Translated by Elizabeth Lutzeier, with Kenneth J. Northcott. Chicago: University of Chicago Press, 1988.

Nissen, Hans J., Peter Damerow, and Robert K. Englund. *Archaic Bookkeeping: Early Writing and Techniques of Economic Administration in the Ancient Near East.* Translated by Paul Larsen. Chicago: University of Chicago Press, 1993.

Oppenheim, A. Leo. *Ancient Mesopotamia: Portrait of a Dead Civilization.* Revised and completed by E. Reiner. Chicago: University of Chicago Press, 1977.

Pollock, Susan. *Ancient Mesopotamia: The Eden That Never Was.* Cambridge: Cambridge University Press, 1999.

Pollock, Susan, and Reinhard Bernbeck, eds. *Archaeologies of the Middle East: Critical Perspectives.* Oxford: Blackwell, 2005.

Postgate, J. Nicholas. *Early Mesopotamia: Society and Economy at the Dawn of History.* London: Routledge, 1994.

Potts, Daniel T. *The Archaeology of Elam: Formation and Transformation of an Ancient Iranian State.* Cambridge: Cambridge University Press, 1999.

Roaf, Michael. *Cultural Atlas of Mesopotamia and the Ancient Near East.* New York: Facts on File, 1990.

Rothman, Mitchell, ed. *Uruk Mesopotamia and Its Neighbors: Cross-Cultural Interactions in the Era of State Formation.* Santa Fe: School of American Research, 2001.

Smith, Adam T. *The Political Landscape: Constellations of Authority in Early Complex Polities.* Berkeley: University of California Press, 2003.

Van de Mieroop, Marc. *A History of the Ancient Near East, ca. 3000–323 B.C.* 2nd ed. Oxford: Blackwell, 2007.

Wiesehöfer, Josef. *Ancient Persia from 550 B.C. to 650 A.D..* Translated by Azizeh Azodi. London: I.B.Tauris, 1996.

Wilkinson, Tony J. *Archaeological Landscapes of the Near East.* Tucson: University of Arizona Press, 2003.

REFERENCE WORKS

Civilizations of the Ancient Near East. Edited by Jack Sasson and others. 4 vols. New York: Charles Scribner's Sons, 1995.

The Encyclopedia of Islam, parts 1–3. Edited by Marc Gaborieau and others. Leiden: Brill, 2007.

The Oxford Encyclopedia of Archaeology in the Near East. Edited by Eric M. Meyers and others. 5 vols. New York and Oxford: Oxford University Press, 1997.

Illustration Credits

Fig. 17. Ernst Heinrich, *Kleinfunde aus den archaischen Tempelschichten in Uruk* (Leipzig, 1936), plate 17a.

Fig. 20. E. Heinrich, *Kleinfunde aus den archaischen Tempelschichten in Uruk* (Leipzig, 1936), plates 3 and 38.

Fig. 21. Anton Moortgat, *Die Kunst des alten Mesopotamien* (Cologne: Du Mont Schauberg, 1967), plate 14.

Fig. 34. *Sumer, Assur, Babylon,* exhibition catalogue, Hildesheim (Mainz: Ph. von Zabern, 1978), nos. 62 and 63.

Fig. 35. Anton Moortgat, *Die Kunst des alten Mesopotamien* (Cologne: Du Mont Schauberg, 1967), fig. 119.

Fig. 36. *Sumer, Assur, Babylon,* exhibition catalogue, Hildesheim (Mainz: Ph. von Zabern, 1978), no. 65.

Fig. 38. C. Leonard Woolley, *Ur Excavations II: The Royal Cemetery* (London: British Museum, 1934), plate 30.

Fig. 39. C. Leonard Woolley, *Ur Excavations II: The Royal Cemetery* (London: British Museum, 1934), plate 128.

Fig. 41. Anton Moortgat, *Die Kunst des alten Mesopotamien* (Cologne: Du Mont Schauberg, 1967), fig. 136.

Fig. 43. Anton Moortgat, *Die Kunst des alten Mesopotamien* (Cologne: Du Mont Schauberg, 1967), fig. 139.

Fig. 44. Anton Moortgat, *Die Kunst des alten Mesopotamien* (Cologne: Du Mont Schauberg, 1967), fig. 155.

Fig, 45. Anton Moortgat, *Die Kunst des alten Mesopotamien* (Cologne: Du Mont Schauberg, 1967), fig. 170.

Fig. 46. Hansjörg Schmid, *Der Tempelturm Etemenanki in Babylon* (Mainz: Ph. von Zabern, 1995), plate 7.

Fig. 48. Henry W. F. Saggs, *The Greatness That Was Babylon* (London: Sidgwick & Jackson, 1962), plate 21b.

Fig. 50. Eva Strommenger and Max Hirmer, *5 Jahrtausende Mesopotamien* (Munich: Hirmer, 1962), plate 170.

Fig. 51. Walter Andrae, *Das wiedererstandene Assur* (Leipzig: J. C. Hinrichs Verlag, 1938), plan at back of book.

Fig. 53. Dominique Collon, *First Impressions: Cylinder Seals in the Ancient Near East* (Chicago: University of Chicago Press, 1987), nos. 548 and 276

Fig. 54. Leonard W. King, *Babylonian Boundary Stones* (London: British Museum, 1912), plate 1.

Fig. 55. Anton Moortgat, *Die Kunst des alten Mesopotamien* (Cologne: Du Mont Schauberg, 1967), fig. 259.

Fig. 58. Charlotte Trümpler, ed., *Agatha Christie and Archaeology* (London: British Museum Press), p. 72.

Fig. 60. Richard D. Barnett and A Lorenzini, *Assyrische Skulpturen* (Recklinghausen: Aurel Bongers, 1975), fig. 130.

Fig. 61. Hansjörg Schmid, *Der Tempelturm Etemenanki in Babylon* (Mainz: Ph. von Zabern, 1995), plate 41.

Fig. 62. Eckhard Unger, *Babylon* (Berlin and Leipzig: W. de Gruyter, 1931), frontispiece.

Fig. 65. Roman Ghirshman, *Perse* (Paris: Gallimard, 1963), fig. 190.

Fig. 66. Roman Ghirshman, *Perse* (Paris: Gallimard, 1963), fig. 283.

Fig. 70. Walter Andrae, *Das wiedererstandene Assur* (Leipzig: J. C. Hinrichs Verlag, 1938), figs. 70 and 81.

Fig. 72. *Sumer, Assur, Babylon,* exhibition catalogue, Hildesheim (Mainz: Ph. von Zabern, 1978), plate 160.

Fig. 74. Oskar Reuther, *Die Ausgrabungen der deutschen Ktesiphon-Expedition 1928/29* (Berlin: Staatliche Museen zu Berlin, 1929), fig. 7.

(All other illustrations are drawings and photographs by the authors or in their possession.)

Index